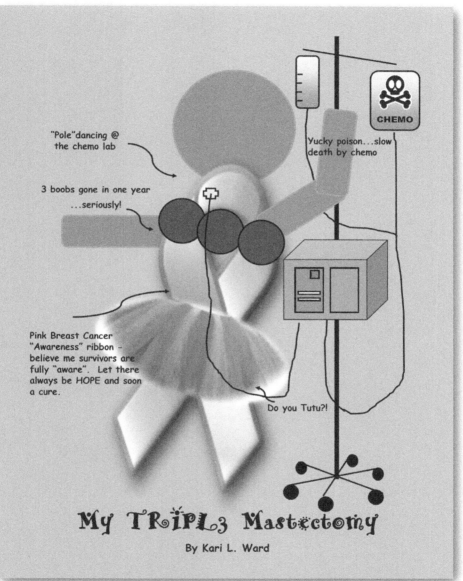

My cover concept of what "my triple mastectomy" may look like.

My Triple Mastectomy

My Triple Mastectomy

KARI L. WARD

Internet addresses contained in this book were correct at the time of publication.
Library of Congress Control Number: 2015902913
CreateSpace Independent Publishing Platform
North Charleston, South Carolina

ISBN-13: 9781508556640
ISBN-10: 1508556644
© 2015 Kari L. Ward
Edited by: Joseph J. Ward
Printed in the United States of America

For JOGJJ-
Thank you for all the ways you bless me. I love you all so much!
I am sorry you had to go through hell and back with me,
but I hope and pray you will always know that
"Nothing can separate us from His love" *(Romans 8:38-39) and*
"He will never leave you nor forsake you" *(Hebrews 13:5).*

J, I love and respect you!
Thank you for all the ways you kept the faith and did not waver.
Thank you for following God's lead for our lives.
Thank you for being the head of our household.
Thank you for loving me and all my imperfections (especially when I was lopsided!).
Thank you for reminding me of the strength we have in Jesus.
And thank you for not once letting go of my hand.

♥K

Daddy, in honor of you!

Contents

A Word from the Author

*B*efore June 6, 2012, I couldn't even spell *mastectomy*. (I still occasionally mispronounce it.) Today, I am all too familiar with the word, its spelling, and the emotions attached to it. Unfortunately, I am only one of far too many women who have had to say good-bye to their "girls."

Everything happens for a reason and ultimately, *"we know that God causes everything to work together for the good of those who love God and are called according to his purpose for them"* (Romans 8:28). I hold on to that promise. Writing this book was therapy for me, and I pray and hope that God gets the glory.

When it felt like my life was falling apart around me, I would find comfort in God's word. I would read and re-read his promises from the Bible and journal what I was going through at the time. Eventually, my notebooks began to fill up and, after about nine months, I decided to start compiling my story. It was about this time that I realized I was going to lose not one…not two…but three boobs in one year! I have tried to use humor in this story to inspire and to encourage but, most of all, to be real.

I wrote this book for both breast cancer patients and their supporting network of family and friends. Time tends to heal all wounds, and occasionally as I reflect on certain aspects of my treatment I catch myself thinking *it wasn't that bad, was it?* But then I re-read my journal entries and realize *yes, it was*! If you or a loved one are facing breast cancer right now, what you are feeling is real. Don't let anyone take your emotions away from you! Let yourself feel every single one of those emotions. But also realize that your race is a marathon and not a sprint. I have an amazing support team that has held up my family and me in prayer and in so many other ways. I will never be able to adequately say thank you to all of them. I pray that you, too, will find your support team.

Many times, my faith has wavered on this journey. I have questioned my precious and holy God. I have gotten mad. I have been selfish. But the whole time, God kept me in the palm of his hand. ***"He lifted me out of the pit of despair, out of the mud and the mire. He set my feet on solid ground and steadied me as I walked along"*** (Psalm 40:2). Through all the highs and lows of this journey, he loved me like crazy. My prayer and hope is that you will know that he is doing the same for you.

I'm not a doctor. Any statistical or medical analyses cited in this book are my layman's interpretation of such. Please don't use *my* story as a reason not to follow sound medical advice since every patient's situation is different.

While I am extremely grateful to all of my doctors, nurses, and medical staff for their amazing dedication, skill, and compassion, I have omitted their names out of respect for the doctor/patient relationship. They made the best decisions they could as my "weirdness" unfolded, even if the results weren't always perfect.

My (Pre-diagnosis) Letter to Cancer

June 6, 2012. About noon.

Dear Cancer,

We have never met personally before now. Yes, you have rudely invaded too many of my family and friends' bodies and, yes, that was personal. But until now, I have been avoiding a personal relationship with you.

Okay, so now that we are introduced, let me take this opportunity to tell you a few things about me.

Don't ever think that I'm going to let you take over my life. I have the power of Christ in me. In fact, **"[His] power is made perfect in [my] weakness"** (2 Corinthians 12:9 NIV).

I'd be lying if I said I wasn't scared, but **"when I am afraid, I will trust in [God]"** (Psalm 56:3 NIV) and **"I will not be afraid for [God is] close beside me"** (Psalm 23:4).

I learned a promise from God when you visited my dad two years ago. He told me, **"Never will I leave you; never will I forsake you"** (Hebrews 13:5 NIV).

So again, I have the power of Christ made perfect in any weakness you insert into my body. Oh, and did I tell you I am a fighter? I have the *full armor of God* accessible whenever I remember to dress in it (Ephesians 6:10-18).

Also:

<u>I am a witness</u>: **"Let the redeemed of the LORD say so"** (Psalm 107:2 KJV). So!

<u>I am a warrior</u>: **"May the praise of God be in their mouths and a double-edged sword in their hands"** (Psalm 149:6 NIV).

<u>I am a bride of Christ</u>: Isaiah 61:10, Isaiah 62:4, and Zephaniah 3:17.

And the best promise of all: **"The LORD will fight for [me]; [I] need only to be still"** (Exodus 14:14 NIV).

And even if you win this battle in my body, my "earthly tent," you can't even come close to touching me in the eternal body God made for me (2 Corinthians 5:1).

So there! My dukes are up. I'm ready to fight! Again, even if you win this earthly fight, Christ has already won the eternal battle. I am His, and He promised a kingdom that is unshakable. For that I am thankful, and I worship my Father God with holy fear and awe (Hebrews 12:28).

Dear Holy Father,

Thank you that I am yours and thank you that you've got me in the palm of your hand. I love you!

"May the words of my mouth and the meditation of my heart be pleasing to you, O LORD, my rock and my redeemer" *(Psalm 19:14). Thank you for the grace, mercy, and forgiveness you give me, and thank you that you gave it all so that a sinner like me could be with you for eternity.*

Introduction

I don't know where to begin this story. Unfortunately, so many women and men know the pain and awkwardness that comes from breast cancer and a mastectomy. I officially learned of my cancer diagnosis at 2:45 P.M. on June 6, 2012, during a call from my primary care provider. (I unwittingly referred to this day as "D-Day," not realizing until months later that June 6 actually *is* D-Day…apologies to all my history teachers!) Believe it or not, I actually wrote my "Letter to Cancer" two hours prior to receiving my diagnosis. God definitely drafted that letter in my mind ahead of time to remind me that his strength is unfailing.

I had women with other cancers tell me how lucky I was to have the "glamorous" kind. Funny, I certainly didn't *feel* lucky. I think what they were trying to say was that my treatment options were very promising since people have become very aware of breast cancer in recent years and have responded in kind with generous donations toward breast cancer research and treatment. Still, no form of cancer should ever be referred to as "glamorous." Up until my diagnosis, I had been healthy my entire life. I'd always been active and loved working out. I'd always been very purposeful about taking care of myself. So I was shocked when the doctor told me I had developed enough cancer in my left breast to cause a dimple. The odd thing was, I had just had a normal mammogram three months earlier. My breast surgeon, who was also in disbelief about the rapid growth of the tumor, went back and checked the earlier mammogram and confirmed that it showed no signs of cancer. Maybe I *was* lucky after all.

Since the cancer was growing so quickly and so aggressively, I decided to be proactive and to have the breast surgeon remove both of my "girls." Most of the breast cancer survivors I consulted with recommended getting a bilateral mastectomy, as opposed to a unilateral one, so that I wouldn't have to deal with a reoccurrence in the other breast down the road. My hubbie was also supportive of that approach. I tried to always remember that my breasts were as much his as they were mine. But not once did he compromise my health over his pleasure. I love him so much.

So, I went ahead with the bilateral mastectomy and six rounds of chemotherapy. Because I was strong and healthy, surgical recovery went very well. Even the first three rounds of chemo went well. In fact, I praise my Almighty Father for protecting me from all the negative side effects of the first three rounds. Chemo's four, five, and six, on the other hand, were the start of my demise. I think that is where I will begin my story...

Therefore we do not lose heart.
Though outwardly we are wasting away,
yet inwardly we are being renewed day by day.
For our light and momentary troubles
are achieving for us
an eternal glory that far outweighs them all.
So we fix our eyes not on what is seen,
but on what is unseen.
For what is seen is temporary,
but what is unseen is eternal.

2 Corinthians 4:16-18 NIV

One

Never Will I Leave You

"Can we make a wig out of this?"

From day one of my diagnosis, I knew God was with me. I felt like a warrior for him, and I felt armed with his divine strength, comfort, and peace. I also naively thought that because I had such a successful surgical recovery and the first three chemotherapy treatments weren't too bad, he would deliver me through all of this. I was convinced

I would soon get back to my life, and he would get all the glory. But during my recovery from chemo four, I had a revelation: I DON'T GET TO DECIDE *HOW* GOD GETS THE GLORY!

That was a hard pill to swallow. I couldn't understand why God wouldn't use me in his story the way *I* wanted. I was praising him, serving him, spending time with him, telling others how amazing he was...why couldn't he let me write my own script?

And then it hit me. I don't get to decide *how* God gets the glory. This life, my friends, is not for our glory. It's his story, not ours, and I had to discover my role in *his* story. I am still very much discovering that role!

Up until chemotherapy four, I had experienced only a few of the milder side effects of the treatments, like digestive issues and metallic mouth. By that point, I had lost every single hair on my body. (See my hair shaving story in Appendix 1.) But for the most part, the negative effects of the chemo hadn't really gotten me down. God had supernaturally protected me. Yay God!

But after chemo four, my body started falling apart. I began experiencing neuropathy in my hands and feet. For those of you unfamiliar with neuropathy, to say that it feels like your fingers and toes have fallen asleep is a gross understatement. Instead, imagine someone putting needles in your hands, fingers, and toes while you are trying to walk or get dressed—and you'll get the picture. Very painful!

In addition to the neuropathy, I developed an ear infection and subsequent ear block that didn't clear up until nine months later. (To this day, the ear block still comes and goes and may actually be lymphedema in my eustachian tube.) Also, my left pinky and ring fingers started swelling. My oncologist was concerned with all of these side effects and sent me to the best specialists to relieve the symptoms. But despite all the medical consultations and additional drugs the doctors put me on, the pain and swelling continued.

The worst side effect from chemo four—one that I didn't even know I had at the time—was anemia. As we all know, the body needs oxygen to survive. Oxygen is transported by the hemoglobin in our red blood cells. Anemic patients have a deficiency in either hemoglobin or red blood cell volume that prevents the efficient transport of oxygen. As a result, anemic patients feel exhausted. I was beginning to feel more and more listless with each passing day. The oncologist had been watching the hemoglobin in my blood drop after each successive chemotherapy treatment, but she didn't know what was causing it. It was common for *white* blood cells to drop as a result of the chemo, which is why I was given a shot of the drug Neulasta after each treatment as a preventative measure. But my white blood cell numbers were always good. It was the drop in my red blood cells that was puzzling. I begged my oncologist, only half-jokingly, for a shot of EPO—the performance enhancing drug that has gotten more than a few professional cyclists in trouble. I promised her I wouldn't compete in any world class sporting events. Unfortunately, she failed to see my humor. "Against FDA guidelines," she said. Instead, I was awarded my very first blood transfusion. Thanks for playing!

I have given lots of blood in the past, but I never thought I would become one of those poor, sick people that would have to rely on someone else's blood to help them get better. Several people told me I would be ready to run up eight thousand feet to the summit of Pike's Peak with the influx of new red blood cells from the transfusion. But I felt worse *after* the new blood than I did before. Adding to my woes, I became severely jaundiced and looked as orange as a pumpkin! And just to add salt to the wound, I lost two bracelets that had been given to me for this cancer fight when they were accidently snipped by the discharge nurse when she was cutting off my hospital band!

My medical assistant friend who specializes in blood told me I probably got bad blood during the transfusion. She said that the blood probably had been handled incorrectly at some point and that the red blood cells may have already been damaged or dead when they got to me. *Great. How does that happen? And how can I request a world class marathoner next time?*

Over the next few days, I gradually started to feel a little better, but not much. The cumulative effects of the chemo were finally starting to catch up to me.

*A*t the end of each chapter, contained between the sideways breast cancer ribbons, I've included journal entries from my caring-bridge.org web page. These entries truly convey my real, and sometimes raw, thoughts and feelings as I progressed on my cancer journey. The pink ribbon has become ubiquitous with breast cancer but, to me, also looks like an ithicus (or "Jesus fish") when it's displayed on its side.

- **Written October 15, 2012, 7:21 A.M.: Round 4 Tuesday**

  "Trust in the LORD with all your heart;
  do not depend on your own understanding.
  Seek his will in all you do,
  and he will show you which path to take" (Proverbs 3:5-6).

  Dear Family and Friends,

  Wow! There is so much I want to say, but I will spare you all the details of these last three weeks. I will sum it up into: GOD IS GOOD AND FAITHFUL ALL THE TIME! PRAISE HIM!

  Please forgive me if I haven't taken your call or returned your e-mail. Please know you do matter to me—to us—and we are soooooooo appreciative of all your encouragement and support. If I can so boldly ask: please keep praying for us. That has been the best gift that you have given us. Truly it is. All the logistical support has been great, too, and very much appreciated and needed. But prayer works, and you all have lifted us and protected us in prayer. THANK YOU! I am praying for you, too, that as you are praying you may have a personal encounter with our GREAT GOD!

  Thank you so very, very, very much. Oh, it's Breast Cancer Awareness Month, ladies. Treat your "girls" to a mammogram— JUST DO IT!

Love you and God bless you.

In Jesus' Precious Love,
Kari

- **Written October 16, 2012, 6:57 A.M.**

What a great *Jesus Calling* today from the sweet breath of our savior! I LOVE, LOVE, LOVE God's perfect timing. Thank You, Father! Here is a little sampling of today's devotion. Read as if Jesus is talking to you...and He is!:

> Look to Me continually for help, comfort, and companionship. Because I am always by your side, the briefest glance can connect you with Me. When you look to Me for help, it flows freely from my presence....
> ...My constant Companionship is the *pièce de résistance:* the summit of salvation blessings. No matter what losses you experience in your life, no one can take away this glorious gift.[1]

Thank you, family and friends, for your constant comfort. Praying for your double blessings.

Love you and God bless you.

In Jesus' Precious Love,
Kari

- **Written October 17, 2012, 7:11 A.M.**

A verse shared with me yesterday by my sweet Holly. Love you, sis, and God bless you.

"In that day the people will proclaim,
'This is our God!
We trusted in him, and he saved us!
This is the LORD, in whom we trusted.
Let us rejoice in the salvation he brings!'" (Isaiah 25:9).

AMEN! Yay God!

Thank you very much for all your prayers. They are working, and I pray for your trusting in God and your rejoicing in His great salvation.

Love you and God bless you.

In Jesus' Precious Love,
Kari

- **Written October 19, 2012, 8:33 A.M.: Praises**

"This prayer was sung by the prophet Habakkuk:
I have heard all about you, LORD.
I am filled with awe by your amazing works.
In this time of our deep need,
help us again as you did in years gone by.
And in your anger,
remember your mercy....
...The mighty deep cried out,
lifting its hands to the LORD....
...yet I will rejoice in the LORD!
I will be joyful in the God of my salvation!
The Sovereign LORD is my strength!
He makes me as surefooted as a deer,
able to tread upon the heights" (Habakkuk 3:1-2,10, 18-19).

As I awoke this morn to the start of a chemo coma, God directed me to this passage:

**"I will thank the LORD because he is just;
I will sing praise to the name of the LORD Most High"**
(Psalm 7:17).

- **Written October 21, 2012, 10:28 A.M.: Upside of Chemo 4!**

Dear Fam and Friends,

This is something I shared with my Praise and Worship Team this morn, but wanted to pass it on to you, too, because God is using you to help me...thank you. The fog is clearing!

I wanted to share with you something God sunk into me this morning. You have all been great encouragers to me, praying for my spirit to remain encouraged and lifted and for me to know how blessed I am through this journey. THANK YOU. I know I don't always get it, and I don't always live out the way God wants me to even when He sends reminders through my bro's and sis' like you. Even though this is a revelation and a knock over the head, I am sure I will fail again. But thank God that He is so patient. I was tickled at how the last song of the worship lineup tonight is "Blessed Be Your Name."

I don't always get HOW BLESSED I am (and my stubborn streak somehow devises a way for me to rebel against people's words when they tell me so—still working on that—sometimes you just have to let me get there). But God's word, penetrating my heart this morning just reminded me that He uses YOU to remind me HOW BLESSED I AM! I apologize if I have not always taken your encouragement, or even rebelled, argued and resented it.

I love you and am truly thankful for how God is using you to help me through this. Thank you.

Here is a sampling of today's *Jesus Calling*. Please read as if Jesus, the one and only, is talking to you, because He is!:

The best response to losses or thwarted hopes is praise: *The Lord gives and the Lord takes away. Blessed be the name of the Lord....*
... Instead of feeling entitled to all these blessings, respond to them with gratitude. Be prepared to let go of anything I take from you, but never let go of My hand![2]

The verse God gave me this morn:

"From the <u>fullness</u> of his grace [something I don't even deserve] **we have <u>all</u> received one <u>blessing</u> after another"** (John 1:16 NIV, emphasis added).

Thank you, Dear Ones, for helping me remember HOW BLESSED I am. Thank You, Father, for BLESSING me so much. May I always remember Your blessings with gratitude and not entitlement.

In Jesus' Precious Love,
Kari

- **Written October 29, 2012, 9:53 A.M.: Prayer Requests Please**

Dear Family and Friends,

I hardly feel like I can ask you to pray for anything else. You have completely blessed me with your prayers thus far, but maybe I can give you some specifics to pray for.

I was completely delusional when I thought I could just blaze through this chemo. I know God can supernaturally protect me from all the negative side effects of the chemo if He wants. He still has protected me from most so PRAISE HIM for that, and even if he doesn't, PRAISE HIM! But maybe He allows some negative side effects to happen for a reason. His thoughts and ways are not mine and His are higher and far beyond anything I could imagine (Isaiah 55:8-9)—a reason that ultimately glorifies Him or is for the good of those who love Him (Romans 8:28). Maybe the Master is chiseling away at this piece of clay, for we are all His master piece (Ephesians 2:10). Chiseling hurts! (Thanks to my pastor and Skit Guys[3] for helping remind me of this.)

Anyway, in the last week or so I have developed neuropathy. Basically, it feels like my hands and feet are asleep all the time. It should go away after chemo; but with two more rounds, that seems like a very long time to me.

I have developed a rash that looks like bug bites. This seems to be cyclical as this is the second time it has appeared after chemo.

I only crapped my pants twice this week, and fortunately it was at home! Never ever trust a fart! Laugh—that *is* funny. I have a new perspective on the patience required with a toddler in potty training!

And the "biggy" to pray for: I boldly ask you to pray that I don't have lymphedema. For the last few weeks, I have had swelling in my left hand on the outer part of my palm and pinky. I have been referred to a physical thera-pist, but in the last week it has gotten worse. I am praying and hoping that it is edema and fluid retention from the chemo and the cancer, but I am also preparing my heart for a new "normal." Anyway, I have been pretty discour-aged this last week, realizing that my life will never go back to the way it was. That's okay—God's got different plans, and I know He will completely heal me of all of this and the cancer. It has just been rough grieving the transformation of this earthly tent.

When I think of all that Jesus went through just so we could have eternal life, this stuff is nothing! Thank you, Jesus!

Whew, I feel better already. Thank you to my wonder-ful husband who has taken his shield of faith and covered me this week, and thank you to all of you that have al-lowed me to just be.

"Yet I will rejoice in the LORD! I will be joyful in the God of my salvation!" (Habakkuk 3:18).

I love you and am thankful for you. Thanks for allowing me to be real and not sugar coat everything. I am really try-ing not to complain or grumble, but I do want to be real.

God bless you! I am praying for you as you pray for me. May God do something totally amazing for you this week. May you notice ALL His beautiful love notes all over the place, and may you know beyond a shadow of a doubt HOW MUCH YOUR HEAVENLY FATHER LOVES YOU and wants a relationship with you through Jesus Christ. Praying for you to feel that love!

In Jesus' Precious Love,
Kari

- **Written November 5, 2012, 4:50 P.M.: Chemo 5 Ready to Rumble and Kick This**

Dear Friends and Fam,

Thank you for your prayers. Keep them coming. It has been challenging as each chemo gets tougher, but nothing that OUR GREAT GOD can't handle. Got this song "Forever Reign" by Hillsong on my brain. Funny, this has been the theme that has been running through my brain on this cancer journey, and our praise and worship pastor played it last night not even knowing that he was going to play it until about an hour before. YAY GOD! It is encouraging me.

I want to take a moment to pray for our country. We've prayed and we've voted, and now we are praying again! Please join us in praying for our country, our country's leaders, and for attitudes of love and unity and team. God bless America!

"May God be merciful and bless us.
May his face smile with favor on us.
May your ways be known throughout the earth,
your saving power among people everywhere.
May the nations praise you, O God.

Yes, may all the nations praise you.
Let the whole world sing for joy,
because you govern the nations with justice
and guide the people of the whole world.
May the nations praise you, O God.
Yes, may all the nations praise you.
Then the earth will yield its harvests,
and God, our God, will richly bless us.
Yes, God will bless us,
and people all over the world will fear him" (Psalm 67).

Dear Beloved God in heaven,

Please give us a president that loves this country and everything it stands for.
Please give us a president who respects You as the one true God.
Please give us a president who will, with Your help, restore this nation to its former glory—the way You created her.
Please help us to respect what You have given to us and not take anything for granted ever again.
Please, God, weaken the evil and strengthen the good.
May our eyes be opened.

In Jesus' Name,
Amen.

God Bless America!

Two

Death by IV

(When I first started writing this chapter, I felt like I was living in a deep, dark hole. I was angry, bitter, and frustrated with being sick. So, please forgive some of the "rawness" this next part conveys.)

At this point, I would have never, ever, wished chemotherapy on my worst enemy. The cancer hadn't done a thing to me besides dimpling my breast, but this chemo stuff was literally killing me. Because of the continuing ear block, I couldn't hear out of my left ear. My left hand and fingers were swollen and in pain all the time. I couldn't keep food down, despite all the anti-nausea drugs that I had been taking. I couldn't sleep and couldn't get out of bed either. My hands, fingers, feet, and toes hurt from the neuropathy. All this, coupled with explosive diarrhea, made the three weeks between chemotherapies four and five miserable. I was sure I was going to die, if not literally at least figuratively, from the almost daily crapping of my pants. I learned all too well to heed the advice of Jack Nicolson's character in the movie *The Bucket List* when he says, "Never trust a fart."[4]

I can't adequately describe chemotherapy. I know everyone's experience is different. Everyone's "cocktail" is different. Not everyone has the same side effects. But for me, beginning with chemo four, it was a living hell. Thankfully, despite how tough it got, God protected me! I had a physical glow about me and had gained ten pounds due to the steroids, so I looked "healthy" to most people, even though I felt horrible. My bald nugget was the only clue that I was still ill. My friends would ask, "What was so bad about chemotherapy? I heard it was just like a really bad flu." Whoa! What an understatement! During those moments, I wished I could have hit them upside the head or even given them a tiny taste of what chemo was like so they could realize how insensitive they were being. Two years earlier, I had made some of the same insensitive statements to my dad during his treatment for stage four lung cancer. It's funny how one's perspective changes on the flip-side. I knew they were attempting to empathize; but trust me, you can never really understand chemo until you've experienced it firsthand.

God bless all the cancer patients and their families that have had to endure this hell! If you are a loved one of someone with cancer (and forgive me if I offend you or overstep my boundaries), please, please don't ever say you understand what chemo is like or that it doesn't sound that bad or that—my all-time favorite—you would handle it better. It is a living hell, especially with each additional treatment. No matter what your chemo cocktail is, you are living through death by IV. (I told you this section was dark!) Here is an excerpt from my journal written November 11, 2012, after my fifth chemotherapy treatment:

Dear Cancer,
How ruthless you are! Maybe you're just a sick joke to see how many hoops I'd jump through-to see how hard I'd fight. Really, you've done nothing to me. Left unattended, yes, you may have reared your ugly head at some point-maybe. How much time could

I have stolen from you? But you forced me to fight for my family-to come head-to-head with chemo-and I'm losing the fight. Chemo, I hate you! You suck so bad! I don't know how you could be the cure. You have pulled me to the depths of hell, and I still have one more round.

Dear God,

I'm sorry my bravado is gone. I'm sorry I'm weaker than I thought. I'm sorry that I just want to be put out of my misery. I was convinced You would use me, You would blaze me through this fire, and You would get all the glory. But I had a revelation: I don't get to decide <u>how</u> You get the glory. I'm sorry. I know Your ways are higher than my ways and Your thoughts are higher than my thoughts. I'm sorry I'm so weak.

Dear Jesus,

I'm sorry you had to endure so much more for a weak, whiny, crybaby like me. Oh Great God, please have mercy on me. Please! I don't question Your goodness. I don't question Your ways. Okay, maybe I do. I'm sorry. But why would You allow everything to be stripped from me: my hair, my sense of touch, my sense of taste, the feeling in my fingers, toes, hands and feet. Why do You allow the swelling and pain in my hands and the deafness from the ear block? Do You know HOW ALONE I feel? I have no control over my bowels. I feel isolated from my family and close friends who just want me to be joyful. I feel like all color and sound have left from this world. Father, what do You want from me? I don't know what to do! I want to praise You, but I don't know how to anymore. I don't know how to honor or serve You. I thought I was doing that. I thought I was living "full-on and all-in" for You. But now I feel all broken up and deserted. I know You promise "never will I leave you; never will I forsake you." I will cling to those words with my last fingernail. I NEED You Father! I can't bear much more of this. I know anyone reading this will think I've completely lost it, and they will probably have me committed. Great-another loss! Father, please, Please, PLEASE protect my Joe. Protect my kids. Please give them a rainbow at the end of this hellish death walk. Thank You for them. They are truly a blessing. I hate that they have to go through this with me. Now, so many things make sense about my dad. I'm sorry, Dad, that I didn't understand this suffering you had all your life, only to have it increase exponentially as your end days drew near. I'm sorry, God. I sit here silently. I just don't know what to say or do anymore. I PRAISE YOU because You are God. You are good! I'm sorry that I just want to sit back for a while and cry, grieve, and mourn my losses. I know I'll get there. Just let me get there. But for now, I just need to grieve.

I was reading the *Hunger Games* trilogy at the time, and I related to the main character, Katniss, in so many ways. In *Mocking Jay*, Katniss experiences intense feelings of loneliness in which she feels neither alive nor dead, as if she's been suspended between the two states inside a caterpillar's cocoon. At first, it's a peaceful condition, but then it becomes suffocating. The wait to transform into a beautiful butterfly becomes excruciating, and nothing can speed up the process.[5]

I related to these sentiments because I knew I had to get out of *my* cocoon all by myself. Just like a month breaking free from its chrysalis, I knew I had to struggle in order to force the blood to my wings to prepare them for flight. In other words, sometimes you just have to do the work, and some roads you have to walk alone.

Normally, I'm not this deep.

So there we were. The side effects from chemotherapy five had been ten times worse that of number four. My husband thought I was going to die. My kids admitted that they thought I was going to die. And I sure felt like I was going to die.

I *had* to get out of chemo six.

My husband and I pretended we were lawyers, brainstorming every possible reason why my oncologist should award me a bye on the last treatment. We knew it would be a tough sell. Doctor C, as I'll refer to her, was aggressive and known for doing what it takes to keep her patients cancer free and out of the hospital. She was big on "standard of care" and would not likely approve skipping the final treatment. Deep down inside, I knew it was *my* decision, but I desperately wanted her approval to forgo the last chemo. Knowing her track record, though, it would take an act of God for her to agree.

I soon realized that *I* was the one who was going to experience the act of God.

The morning of chemo six, I awoke with such peace and with certain Bible passages on my mind. ***"Be strong and courageous, and <u>do the work</u>. Don't be afraid or discouraged, for the LORD God, my God, is with you. He will not fail you or forsake you"*** (1 Chronicles 28:20, emphasis added). I love this verse because it demands action: *do the work*. And there was another verse in my head that morning: *"Be still, and know that I am God!"* (Psalm 46:10). I have to admit, I struggle with being still. I'm a "doer," an organized task master. As a mother of four and with a husband who travels half the week, being still is quite the challenge! Maybe that's why God allowed my anemia. "I'll just take the batteries out of her," I can hear him saying! As much as I knew I had to do the work, I knew I had to be still, too.

But the Bible doesn't stop there. *"The LORD will fight for you; you need only to be still"* (Exodus 14:14 NIV). Okay, another verse telling me to be still! I could picture God telling me, "Be still, Kari. Be still." And if you add in the preceding verse: *"Do not be afraid. Stand firm and you will see the deliverance the LORD will bring you today. The Egyptians you see today you will never see again. The LORD will fight for you; you need only be still"* (Exodus 14:13-14 NIV).

Something clicked in my brain when I considered the context of these passages. You see, at this point in the Book of Exodus, Moses was leading his people out of slavery in Egypt toward the Promised Land. But there was one little problem. They were being chased by Egyptian soldiers who were pretty peeved that they had escaped. And now, Moses and the Israelites were surrounded by mountains on both sides of them and the Red Sea in front. They were trapped. It's at this point that God commanded Moses to stand firm and be still. But instead of coming down in the form of fire and brimstone to exact judgment on the Egyptians himself, God tells Moses to do it. *"Why are you crying out to me? Tell the Israelites to move on. Raise your staff and stretch out your hand over the sea to divide the water so that the Israelites can go through the sea on dry ground"* (Exodus 14:15-16 NIV). Have faith and take the next step. Do the work. It was clear God was telling me to go ahead with the chemo.

There was one final verse that popped into my head in the hours leading up to chemo six. *"Whatever you do, do well. For when you go to the grave, there will be no work or planning or knowledge or wisdom"* (Ecclesiastes 9:10). In other words, every breath is a gift!

God gave me such a tremendous sense of peace on that day. I barely put up a fight when, as predicted, Doctor C recommended gutting out the final chemotherapy treatment. Since my vital signs were all okay to proceed, we decided this was the "work" I was supposed to do. I would take the first step, be still, and let the Lord fight for me.

And he did.

Chemo six was supposed to be the doosey, the culmination of all the poisons surging through my body. I don't know why I didn't expect this to happen but, sure enough, God divinely protected me from the negative side effects! The hair that had already started growing back stayed. No sickness. The achiness and flu-like symptoms didn't show up. The explosive diarrhea was very minimal.

Months earlier, we had tentatively planned a trip to Disneyland to celebrate the end of chemo, and I actually felt like going. After all, our Holy Father had given me a gift, and I didn't want to waste it. God was allowing me to feel really good with a lot of energy. It was a gift we had to take advantage of right then and there.

- **Written November 14, 2012, 3:32 P.M.: Thankful That This Sickness Will Not End In Death**

As my dad would say, "Uff-da!" This is a doosey of an update, so brace yourselves.

C.S. Lewis wrote in his book *The Great Divorce*:

If we insist on keeping Hell (or even Earth) we shall not see Heaven: if we accept Heaven we shall not be able to retain even the smallest and most intimate souvenirs of Hell. I believe, to be sure, that any man who reaches Heaven will find that what he abandoned (even in plucking out his right eye) has not been lost: that the kernel of what he was really seeking even in his most depraved wishes will be there, beyond expectation, waiting for him in the 'High Countries'…I think earth, if chosen instead of Heaven, will turn out to have been, all along, only a region in Hell: and earth, if put second to Heaven, to have been from the beginning a part of Heaven itself.[6]

Whew! This has been a rough go with chemo. Praise the Lord for you. I am so thankful for your prayers through this. For those of you who have had to deal with my whining all week: thank you for your patience. I am starting to physically feel better, and I think (and you'll have to ask my hubbie to be sure) I made it over the emotional/psychological chemo brain of a couple days ago. Thank You, Lord! Again, thank you so much for covering my family and me in prayers.

C.S. Lewis' passage above really challenged my thinking this last week. But as my worship pastor is always saying, if we know Jesus, we are living in eternity right now. And with that truth, I don't want to curl up on the side lines and let this crappy chemo get the best of me. I'll curl up in a ball but only to roll with the punches!

We have been praying for a little four-year-old girl named Emma that has cancer. Her mom asked on her CaringBridge page the other day if her little daughter's suffering was necessary. Why would God allow a *child* to get cancer? This godly woman deduced that, even though she didn't completely understand it, her family's suffering brought them closer to God and gave them the boldness necessary to talk to others about Christ. She spoke of the peace of knowing that God is in control and the privilege of being able to suffer for Him.

Wow! I cannot even begin to tell you how much comfort and peace this has given me in my own suffering. Thank You, God, for connecting us with this precious family. I can't even imagine what it is like for them as parents to have to see their little baby go through this. Thank You, Holy Spirit, for helping me see these truths and the strength and encouragement You give me. Thank You, God, for the suffering. I praise Your Holy Name!

So one more chemo: November 27th. I know it may appear from the outside that these six rounds have seemed like something I have just had to check off, and I thank you for cheerleading from the sidelines. But from on the inside, they have been hell. Really, no sugar coating it. I don't think I could ever do chemo again unless it was God's will. To some, that may sound selfish. But the way I look at it, chemo has stolen enough time from me already. In the book of Ecclesiastes, it's stated (I think five times) that we should eat, drink, and enjoy the fruits of our labor. Chemo does not fall into any of those categories. If I hadn't done the chemo, I wouldn't understand the real suffering of it. I am just sorry I didn't understand this better when my dad was going through it. I really don't know how people who endure hundreds of rounds of chemo can keep doing it. (Only through Christ who gives them strength!) But what about those who don't know Christ? I don't know why I thought God was going to let me blaze through all these rounds of chemo. I had a revelation last week, I don't get to decide *how* God gets the glory. I am merely a servant in His story.

Thanks for enduring my chemo brain and my long update.

Again, thank you for everything, God has been using you to provide for our needs just as we need them. I can't tell you what a lesson in patience this has been for a "control-plan-weeks-in-advance-freak" like myself. Ah, the refining process.

Love you and God bless you!

"So I concluded there is nothing better than to be happy and enjoy ourselves as long as we can. And people should eat and drink and enjoy the fruits of their labor, for these are gifts from God" (Ecclesiastes 3:12-13).

"Jesus told her, 'I am the resurrection and the life. Anyone who believes in me will live, even after dying. Everyone who lives in me and believes in me will never ever die. Do you believe this, Martha?'" (John 11:25-26)

- **Written November 24, 2012, 12:52 P.M.: Thankful**

Just a nobody,
wanting everybody,
to know a SOMEBODY (Jesus that is)!

Happy belated Thanksgiving!

We escaped for the week to celebrate life, birthdays, and my pending sixth, and final, chemo. (The word "chemo" makes me shudder since I never really recovered from number five.) The last one is on Tuesday, and for that I am very thankful.

One of my friends, and two time breast cancer survivor, has really helped me pull through this season. I just want to humbly ask for your prayers during this next year as my body starts from ground zero to become healthy again. I had no idea how stripped and diminished my body would get, but I know that this "tent" is temporary.

After the chemo is done, I'll still be visiting the cancer center every three weeks until August for Herceptin, but the side effects won't be anything like the chemo. Thank You, God!

I was spending time with God this morn, and He led me again to this:

"And let us run with endurance the race God has set before us. We do this by keeping our eyes on Jesus, the champion who initiates and perfects our faith. Because of the joy awaiting him, he endured the cross, disregarding its shame. Now he is seated in the place of honor beside God's throne. Think of all the hostility he endured from sinful people; then you won't become weary and give up. After all, you have not yet given your lives in your struggle against sin" (Hebrews 12:1-4).

Because of joy, Jesus endured it ALL for a hostile, ungrateful, arrogant, sinner like me.

Jesus, I am so sorry I have been so angry with how my body has betrayed me. I am sorry I haven't praised You in the bad as well as in the good. I am sorry. Thank You for forgiving me, loving me, and always being with me. Thank You for all that are praying for my fam and me, and I pray for each and every one of them for their safety and protection and health and a supernatural encounter with You. I pray that as we enter this Christmas season that we remember the JOY!

God bless you and yours. You will never know how grateful I am for all the prayers, love, and support you are giving us.

In Jesus' Precious Love,
Kari

- **Written November 29, 2012, 1:31 P.M.: Chemo 6 Administrated**

Praise the Father for who He is and what He has done!

Chemo six went as scheduled. I still have a long week of getting some tests/scans done since the last two chemotherapies have knocked me on my a#$, but I am confident and TRUST JESUS that I will be feeling better soon.

Please continue to pray for supernatural healing and protection as we get through these next two and a half weeks so that I can officially say DONE with chemo!

Love you and God bless you.

In Jesus' Precious Love,
Kari

- **Written December 8, 2012, 2:30 P.M.: Up for Air**

FINALLY up for air and, oh man, does it smell so sweet! Thanks for ALL your prayers. God is good. PRAISE HIM ALL THE TIME!

My youngest was singing the song "This Life" by Mercy Me all day the other day—what a great reminder of how to live.

Merry Christmas and God bless you and, again, THANK YOU for all your prayers. I will continue on with Herceptin every three weeks until August, and I start Tamoxifin for maybe the next ten years.

I cannot even begin to tell you how good it feels to know that I won't have to put any more chemo in my body. I think that in itself is healing my body. YAY GOD!

Thank you, thank you, thank you, for your prayers. We love you and we are praying for your joyous Christmas. Love truly heals!

Dance Party Fun!

Three

DISNEY

K & J on their way to Disney!

*W*ith all six chemotherapy treatments behind us, off we went to Disneyland! We took the kids out of school in mid-December and headed to California for the week.

The kids were completely surprised. We waited until a few days before our trip, on December 6, to tell them. Ever since I was a kid, we've celebrated the Feast of Saint Nicholas on this night by putting out our shoes for Saint Nick to fill with candy, usually gold chocolate coins. This year, however, Saint Nick put some Disney gift cards in the kids' shoes along with a note to "celebrate life"—a nod to all their hard work after the last couple arduous months.

Every family should enjoy Disneyland at least once in their lives. It truly is a special, magical place and a great place to start healing. It was beautifully decorated for Christmas. The weather was nice. And God gave me supernatural energy. We went hard for three and a half days, and I wasn't even the limiting factor! I felt strong. I rode all the rides again and again.

Being able to enjoy all the attractions at Disney was very special for me. You see, the preceding summer we hosted a Colorado family reunion three weeks after my double mastectomy. It was great to see everyone, and I was very happy that the family could partake in a lot of high adventure activities like the amusement park, horseback riding, hot springs pool, and vapor caves in Glenwood Springs. As for me— well, I couldn't do any of those things since I was still recovering from surgery. And this girl has a hard time sitting on the sidelines (although I did sit the bench for much of my high school basketball career!). Normally, I have no problem occasionally volunteering to watch every-one's purses or to keep an eye on the little kids. But it was much more challenging when the role was forced upon me. It was sheer torture for me to go to an amusement park and water park and not be able to "play." My selfish side wanted to flee from the family activities, to stay in bed, or to find something else to do. But the side of me that loves my family and wants to witness their happiness and enjoyment, forced me to dry those tears and to go watch them have fun—and cry about it later. I'm so grateful that our Heavenly Father lets us crawl up into his lap and weep. It's in this position that he comforts us and gives us the strength to move on.

So back to Disney. I could ride all the rides, swim, go into the hot tub, workout—all activities I had set aside the last few months. It's funny how little things like swimming don't seem to matter until they are tak-en away from you. I know everyone is different, but one of the hardest things for me throughout this whole process was not being able to participate, to "be still."

Disney rocked! I still didn't have much hair so I used hats and wigs to keep my head warm—and to not embarrass my two "tween"-agers. I don't care what anyone says. It's hard seeing a grown woman, especially your mom, with a peach-fuzzed nugget! Thankfully, my combination of scarfs and hats managed to withstand all the rides, even the upside-down roller coaster California Screamin'!

I had learned my lesson about "wig security" a few months earlier. Shortly after I started chemo on one of the first weekends I didn't have any hair, a guy at church thought he'd be cute and tug on the end of my wig. (I'm not kidding. Someone really did this!) He knew I was as bald as they come under my nice, sun-highlighted wig, but I guess he didn't care for it because he sarcastically said "nice hair" as he pulled. I don't think he was *trying* to embarrass me but was joking around since the hair obviously wasn't my own. But I wasn't ready to sport the Telly Savalas look in public just yet. And joking or not, don't *ever* mess with a bald lady's wig! Thankfully, I reacted quickly enough to grab my head before being exposed because I don't think the wig was tight enough to withstand his tug. It was a recycled wig from the American Cancer Society and had certainly seen better times.

We returned home from Disneyland the day before my birthday. Talk about a great birthday present—we had already been celebrating for a whole week! They say that after you're diagnosed with cancer that every birthday becomes more special. I'm not sure I wholly agree. Maybe it's my "chemo brain" or maybe it's because there is a part of me that still doesn't feel like a "survivor," even as of this writing. Anyway, we normally celebrate birthdays in my family for weeks, and mine was not going to be the exception! Granted, a week at Disneyland was a lot more luxurious than what we normally did for birthdays, but this was a "We Survived Chemo" present, darn it, and the party was going to continue!

The next night our church treated us to the Broadmoor Hotel's Christmas dinner and show as part of the annual staff holiday party. Amazing! And to top it off, our very generous friends booked us a room at the five star resort—and paid for it. Maybe I had died and gone to heaven already!

Indeed, the entire Christmas season was full of blessings. The next Sunday, the children rocked our church's Christmas service. This had been my third straight year for designing and directing the program, and God had always given me clear instructions on what to do. One of my fellow cancer survivor friends had warned me not to direct the program this year because of how listless I would feel after chemo. I considered her advice, but deep down inside I knew that if God ordained it he would make it happen. And he did! *Praise you, Father.* It was amazing! My oldest daughter helped me direct and did a fantastic job for an eleven-year-old.

The rest of the Christmas season was wonderful, restful, adventurous, and protected by God. We skied, played in the snow, went sledding, ice skated, hung out, and celebrated Jesus' birthday by giving thanks and glory to God for the miracle of healing. Even though I had lost all my eyebrows and eyelashes and had a peach-fuzzed nugget, at last I was starting to feel better and heal. Soon I would be back to my old self—or so I thought.

J and I getting ready to go out to a Christmas party.

Team Ward
Christmas 2012

What my head really looked like: peach fuzz, drawn on
eyebrows, and no eyelashes (only eyeliner).

- **Written December 25, 2012, 5:02 P.M.: Merry CHRISTmas!**

Dear Family and Friends,

Merry Christmas! Thank you for the gift of prayer and support during these last six months. This has definitely been a very blessed Christmas for us. Sorry we didn't get Christmas cards out this year. We have LOVED looking at yours. We still want to wish you all a Merry Christmas and a blessed New Year. We are very blessed because of you. Thank you! May you know how much your Heavenly Father loves you.

"'May the LORD bless you
and protect you.
May the LORD smile on you
and be gracious to you.

**May the LORD show you his favor
and give you his peace'"** (Numbers 6:24-26).

Four

A WALK IN THE PARK

January was going to be the month I got my new boobs—a late Christmas present. I was so excited! I had always been a big-chested gal, and for most of my adult life I had actually wanted *smaller* breasts. I like to run, but wearing four sports bras at once to keep my "girls" from flopping around is kind of a drag! So, for this final phase of my breast reconstruction, the surgeon was going to put in permanent implants to give me a slightly smaller, albeit perkier, chest.

Compared to the double mastectomy, this operation was supposed to be a breeze. The surgeon really downplayed the seriousness of the procedure. *Open me up, take the skin expanders out, put the implants in, and sew me back up.* That's it! No drains, no narcotics, and back to work the next day.

I only told a few people about my upcoming surgery. One of my friends remarked how the date of my surgery was the same day as Victoria's Secret's semi-annual bra sale. *Maybe a stop by the mall on the way home?* I was pretty cavalier about the whole thing. In fact, in the days leading up to the surgery, I didn't make a point of setting up post-op help for my family or having people pray. After all, it was going to be quick and easy. "I got this," I thought.

I should have known that, for me, it wouldn't be that simple. I had had two previous operations in my life in which I was anesthetized, and after both of them I saw a vision of Jesus as I was waking up afterward. In the first experience, Jesus had his arms outstretched and a brilliant light radiated around him. It was so real I could feel his warmth and peace. The second time, my husband Joe and I were sitting in Jesus' lap, and he had his arms around us. Both instances were beautiful. This time, however, I didn't see Jesus when I came to. Instead, I woke up crying because I missed him. *What happened?*

It took me a few days to mourn this. I couldn't understand. Had I arrogantly thought that since this was such an "easy" surgery I didn't need him? *Oh, Jesus. I am sorry. I didn't think—I didn't mean it—Jesus, I need you always!*

Within the next few weeks, I started walking briskly in accordance with my post-surgical recovery regimen. Every time I did, though, I would get really tired, really quickly. I hadn't worked out since the start of December, but I didn't think that taking one month off would make me feel that out of shape. Prior to my last chemo, I had been running, swimming, cycling, and lifting weights.

I decided to take it easy and to be more sedentary. But by the end of January, I had a hard time even getting out of bed. I was exhausted and had no energy.

I found out why at my oncologist visit on February 19. I immediately could tell something was wrong by Doctor C's reaction when she looked at my latest lab results. She kept mumbling something like, "What are we going to do with you? I don't know why your blood keeps falling."

In a nutshell, blood tests showed that my hemoglobin had dropped to 6.9 grams per deciliter of blood. This was the lowest it had ever been, even before the blood transfusion in the fall. Normal hemoglobin for women is about 12-14 g/dl, and doctors start to get nervous if it drops below 9. At a 6.9, I was *severely* anemic. What was so disheartening is that I was expecting my numbers to improve since it had been several weeks since my last chemo. I really thought I was starting to heal. But, for some reason, my hemoglobin continued to drop and my body simply wasn't getting the oxygen it needed. "Maybe it's your bone marrow," my oncologist said. "You need to have a bone marrow biopsy. I think it's in your bone marrow. But first, we have to get you to the hospital for some new blood."

Before I knew what hit me, I was being whisked off to the hospital for *another* blood transfusion. I have to admit, I was really scared. My husband Joe was already on his way to the Denver airport for a business trip and didn't answer his phone. Panic struck. I didn't know if I was dying. I didn't know if they needed to do the bone marrow biopsy right then. I just didn't know.

Thank God I was greeted by a few sweet nurses on the tenth floor of the hospital who helped calm me down. One said, "Girl, you don't look like a six!" referring to my low hemoglobin number. I guess at a 6.9, I'm not supposed to come charging in on the phone with my hubbie and with a smile on my face! I was definitely huffing and puffing, though. The nurses' whole demeanor made me relax and take a deep breath. *I'm not going to die, at least not right now.* Joe had just called back. He'd gotten excused from his trip and had turned back from the airport to join me at the hospital. Soon, he and our pastor arrived at the hospital to pray me through another transfusion.

The blood transfusion was the band aide I needed. It raised my hemoglobin to 9.5.

Unfortunately, it didn't last. My numbers were already dropping a week later when I showed up for the bone marrow biopsy. Right about this time, Robin Roberts of Good Morning America had just come back to work after her long and solitary treatment for *myelodysplastic syndrome*, a condition which often causes bone marrow failure. She had to endure a painful bone marrow transplant and a month in the hospital—two things I absolutely wanted to avoid. But, praise the Lord, the results of the biopsy came back favorable. I had healthy bone marrow. One of my friends and a fellow breast cancer survivor had prayed, "May Kari's bone marrow dance!" And it certainly was. Praise you, Father, for dancing bone marrow!

The question then became: if it wasn't my bone marrow then what *was* causing the anemia? Every test and lab result indicated my body was trying very hard to heal, but something was preventing it. I was making plenty of red blood cells, but they kept disappearing. Did I have a vampire problem?

I kept thinking back to my last oncologist appointment with Doctor C. Because she thought my anemia was so severe and wanted to get me over to the hospital as quickly as possible for the blood transfusion, she never saw the blister that had developed at the incision site on my right breast. I didn't think the blister was related to the anemia. Besides, I had an appointment to see my plastic surgeon, Doctor G, that very day, and I figured I would just discuss the blister with him then. It had been five weeks since my "routine" reconstructive surgery and, I realize now, my new breasts should have been healing faster—and certainly shouldn't have developed a blister. Unfortunately, since I unexpectedly went to the hospital for the blood transfusion, I had to cancel the plastic surgery appointment. At the time, the blood transfusion seemed like it took precedence over my boob blister, anyway, so I wasn't particularly concerned with missing my appointment with Doctor G. I should have been.

- **Written January 20, 2013, 2:28 P.M.: We Have a Spirit of Power, Love, and Self Discipline**

Happy New Year, Dear Ones!

Sorry it has been awhile since I have updated you on what is going on with me. Truthfully, after the last chemo eight weeks ago, I felt like a bomb went off and I have been trying to pick up all the pieces. Throw the holidays, school, and activities starting back up in there and, well, it has been interesting. Oh, yeah—let's not forget chemo brain, too.

So, this is what is going on with my treatment. I go every three weeks for Herceptin. The cool thing is that Herceptin is not a chemo, it doesn't make me sick, and I'm only at the cancer center an hour and a half instead of five! So, that is such a bonus.

I also started taking a little white pill called Tamoxifin for the next five-plus years. The sucky thing about this drug is that—as if the chemo hadn't done enough damage to my ovaries and shut them down—this drug definitely will. Cool thing: no more periods! Bad thing: menopause and hot flashes. Cool thing about hot flashes, I am always cold (I had no idea how much insulation hair gave me) so these things definitely warm me up, and so far I have only experienced them in the comfort of my own bed at night.

The reconstruction is still in progress. I had my "switch out" surgery last Monday (in other words, the doctor took out the skin expanding "water balloons" and put the implants in). It went well and I love the plastic surgeon. He's an artist, although my canvas still has a few more procedures and time until it's done. I am excited for what I may get in the area of the breast department. Too bad the insurance company won't throw in a tummy tuck just for good measure. Right now, with all the swelling in my pecs, I'm just trusting that I won't always look like the hulk.

Okay, so the above humor has been absent for a while. I really have been struggling with not feeling well, not looking well, and not being well. It took a friend telling me that I have been "distant" to wake me up. Also, I was inspired by a youth in my church who shared with the congregation one of the verses he memorized: ***"Consider it pure joy, my brothers, whenever you face trials of many kinds, because you know that the testing of your faith develops perseverance. Perseverance must finish its work so that you may be mature and complete, not lacking anything"*** (James 1:2-4 NIV).

In addition, I had a conversation with God this morning while I walked. As I was asking Him about His verse that ***"[His] power is made perfect in weakness"*** (2 Corinthians 12:9 NIV)—and since I have been so weak lately—I wondered where His perfect power has been and why I haven't witnessed it in *my* weakness. He reminded me that, yes, His power is made perfect in my weakness, but that I haven't exactly tried to access it lately. Instead, I've been slathering myself with pity, and letting Satan isolate me in my selfishness and sickness. In short, I've been allowing the devil to steal my joy. God also reminded me of a verse in 2 Timothy 1:7 that says, ***"For God has not given us a spirit of fear and timidity, but of power, love, and self-discipline."*** Alright, dukes back up.

I have not been putting on my "Full Armor of God." Folks (that is such a Midwest term, isn't it?), we have to put that armor on every day, or we are toast.

Anyway, I am so thankful for my husband who has been praying for me, rolling with the punches (especially the menopause ones—please pray for him), and reminding me of God's truths.

So remember at the beginning when I said I was trying to pick up the pieces after the bomb went off? Well, God also reminded me of the first part of that verse about perfect power: ***"But he said to me, 'My grace is sufficient for you, for my power is made perfect in weakness'"*** (2 Corinthians 12:9 NIV). Sometimes we just need to let the pieces fall and always trust that His grace is all we need, period dot.

I apologize to any of you that I have distanced myself from. I thank those of you who have helped me pick myself up this week as my emotions and moods have gotten onto mother nature's roller coaster, and I thank all of you that have been continually reminding me of God's truths, whether by word or actions.

Love you and praying for you and your family. Thank you for your continued prayers, support, and encouragement.

In Jesus' Precious Love,
Kari

- **Written February 19, 2013, 6:46 P.M.: Abnormality for Christ**

Today was supposed to be my tenth (out of seventeen or eighteen) Herceptin treatments, but when my oncologist came in the office and I asked her how she was, she responded, "Fine, but you are not."

For the last few months, I've been anemic but holding out at a good 8.6. Today, for some reason, my hemoglobin dropped to 6.9 (and this explains why I am more tired now than I was after chemo). I was told to go over to the hospital immediately for a blood transfusion and to reschedule treatment.

Joe's work is AMAZING! I got ahold of Joe before he left on a trip this morn. His boss told him to turn around and go home to be with his wife, and then sent me flowers. I LUV Southwest Airlines! They really and truly take care of their people.

So, the transfusion went well. Hopefully in the next twenty four hours I will feel better. I guess I was very shocked to see the drop. I asked if she had transposed the numbers and it was really a 9.6, but it was all highlighted in red and all these bells and whistles were going off. Oh, wait. That was the panic of my onco! She is frustrated. She has never had this happen to a patient. Surely some onco out there has seen this, though, and they will be able to figure out why my red blood cells are not cooperating. I have always done things opposite or different than the norm, so it really doesn't surprise me that this is happening. The next step is a bone marrow biopsy.

I have a great peace. I KNOW God has me. I KNOW it. I KNOW He is using this for something I will never understand, and I trust in His ways. I KNOW that He is healing me, on His timing—not per the statistical norm. I KNOW He is taking care of my family and me, and I am blessed by that.

If I could humbly ask you to please continue to pray for us. That is the biggest way we have been helped through all of this. Thank you for your sincere love in this season. I will never be able to express the gratitude I have for all of you, but I pray that you know how much you are loved and appreciated. I pray that God has been real and evident in your lives as you petition for us.

I have heard this song a lot lately by Plumb, "God I Need You Now." It's a really great song. We need our Savior every minute of every day. He always gives us the strength we need.

God bless you and love you.

In Jesus' Precious Love,
Kari

P.S. Ironically, I got accepted to do the Iron Girl Triathlon under the Team Courage program in August. (Funny, red blood cells are made by iron levels in the body, and my levels are really high. My body is just not taking the iron and making red blood cells, or something else is destroying them.) At this point, I can't even imagine doing one event, much less all three, but that is a goal that is set before me, and **"I can do everything through Christ, who gives me strength"** (Philippians 4:13).

- **Written February 20, 2013, 12:10 A.M.: BLESSED**

My Joe is pretty AMAZING, too! Thank you, J, for making a scary day peaceful and even fun. I LOVE YOU and God bless you!

K

Five

The 4% Club?

*H*erceptin. I wish I could explain my range of emotions when I hear or say or read this word. It is a wonderful drug for those of us whose breast cancer is **H**uman **E**pidermal growth factor **R**eceptor **2**-positive, or HER2+. The HER2 protein is a normal component of everyone's cells. For me, my body was making too much of it which caused the cancer to grow quickly and aggressively. Herceptin works by causing the body to slow its production of the HER2 protein.

Herceptin has come a long way. Each subsequent version has become smarter and more targeted so that it doesn't destroy the good things in our bodies. Herceptin is not a chemotherapy but instead is referred to as an *immunotherapy*. Immunotherapy uses your body's natural immune system to fight the disease and/or lessen treatment-related side effects.

Herceptin patients typically receive one dose of the drug, usually administered intravenously, every three weeks for a year. Normally, it is started simultaneously with chemotherapy treatments. For the first treatment, the chemo nurse infuses it slowly to make sure there are no adverse reactions. As far as I knew, I had never had a reaction and tolerated the Herceptin just fine during chemo. My oncologist suspected that my anemia was caused by the chemotherapy, a well-documented side effect. Indeed, after I had finished all my chemotherapy treatments, the next two Herceptin-only treatments seemed to go well with no side effects, seemingly confirming her theory. My hemoglobin numbers hadn't improved much, but they weren't getting worse either, holding steady in the mid-8 range.

Things changed after my ninth Herceptin treatment at the end of January. All of a sudden, it felt like my body was falling apart. It was around this time that I developed the blister on my right breast.

As you recall, my tenth Herceptin treatment on February 19 was postponed because of the unexpected blood transfusion, so I went back a couple days later to give it another shot. I already had an appointment that day for my "Survivor Class" and, since I was already going to be at the cancer center, I asked if we could do the make-up Herceptin treatment that day, too.

At a Survivor Class, you get a certificate for completing your cancer treatments. This seemed funny to me since I would still be getting Herceptin for another six months, but I don't make the rules! In the class, a nurse practitioner reminds you to eat healthy, live healthy, and make healthy choices—all to keep your cancer in remission. My family and friends will laugh when they read this, but I could have taught the class. You see, prior to my cancer diagnosis I was in picture perfect health. I worked out and ate healthy food for the most part. In fact, at the time I was juicing to detoxify my body from the pollutants so prevalent in our food supply today.

In hindsight, I have a new theory about health: maybe I should have put *more* preservatives and junk in my body and not worked out as much. Maybe then the poisonous chemotherapy drugs wouldn't have been such a shock to my system. Just a theory. After all, God tells us at least five times in Ecclesiastes to eat, drink, and enjoy the fruits of our labor.

I have no regrets about how I've lived my life. I've eaten as healthy as I could and generally taken care of myself, but I also occasionally drink vino with dinner and beer in the hot tub, eat junk food, and regress into sloth mode. If anything, cancer has taught me how little time we have on this earth and that *every* breath is a gift. My new mantra: a girl's gotta live! Pass the scotch and stogie, please! But I digress.

At my Survivor Class, I finally had the chance to show the nurse practitioner the blister on my incision. At this point, the incision itself had started to rip open, too. Right away, the nurse practitioner called the oncologist, Doctor C, to have a look. She scheduled me for an ultrasound to make sure the blister wasn't an abscess and notified the on-call plastic surgeon.

The plastic surgeon drained and stitched the incision and started me on antibiotics to ward off infection. He also took a culture of the fluid that came from the blister to make sure nothing weird was growing there.

The following week, I saw my regular plastic surgeon, Doctor G. He was completely perplexed that the incision had ripped open, but agreed that my severe anemia *could* have caused it. Doctor G re-cut open the whole incision, emptied the fluid from it, and put a drain in. I was amazed that he did all this in his office using only a local anesthetic. I have to admit, it's pretty cool when your surgeon and nurse call you "tough" as they are poking a hole in your skin for a drain. But next time, give me the anesthesia!

Doctor G then sent me over to his friend at the infectious disease center, Doctor D. So far, the culture drawn the week before hadn't grown anything suspicious like a staph infection, but it did show signs of a bacterium called *gram-positive bacillus.* For that reason, Doctor D wanted to treat me with a heavy intravenous antibiotic called Cubicin. He thought that if he could control potential infections, we could save the breast implant. If it became infected, the implant would most likely have to be removed to effectively treat the infection.

Doctor D was cool and calm. He leveled with me from the get-go saying, "Infections disease doctors are pessimistic." He gave it a 50/50 chance that I could keep the implant.

For the next four weeks, I saw at least one of my three doctors almost daily: Doctor C the oncologist, Doctor G the plastic surgeon, and Doctor D the infectious disease doc. Since my antibiotics were administered intravenously, I had to go to the infectious disease center every day. My oncologist wanted more tests and labs done to figure out what was causing the anemia, and the plastic surgeon wanted to keep an eye on the new incision and drain.

On days with no appointments, I stayed in my pajamas. My four-year-old daughter and I just vegged since I was too tired from the anemia to do anything else. My nurse friends were great. They came to my house on weekends and on their days off to administer the antibiotic so I wouldn't have to make the forty two mile round trip to the infectious disease center every day. Eventually, I had them teach me how to do it myself.

Doctor D thought the course of antibiotics was helping. He reassured me by saying, "It looks like we're going to nurse this puppy back to health."

Still, no one knew what was causing my anemia. In my own research I discovered that 4 percent of patients on Herceptin develop low red and/or low white blood cell counts accompanied by fever, chills, and achiness.[7] *Hmm, I had those symptoms the last two times I was given Herceptin.* Oddly, my oncologist wasn't ready to believe that I was part of that tiny 4 percent minority. In the fifteen plus years that the cancer center had been administering Herceptin to thousands of patients, no one had ever developed extreme anemia from the drug. But I was beginning to believe that I was, indeed, a member of the lucky 4 percent club.

I wanted to take a three to six week break from the Herceptin treatments to test my theory that it was causing my anemia. My oncologist disagreed, and she had the facts to back up her recommendation to continue. In clinical studies, Herceptin had been proven to reduce cancer reoccurrences by 46 percent. Forty six percent! That's a huge number for a cancer patient. For that reason, she recommended continuing the treatment but with a reduced dosage. I agreed. After all, I had to trust the experts. On a side note, since my red blood cells had continued to fall in the last three weeks, I was sent back to the hospital for *another* blood transfusion. It seemed like I was in a vicious cycle.

Since I have problems with blindly accepting and being still, I had to do more of my own research. I came across a French study that compared a patient's duration of Herceptin treatments to the probability of cancer reoccurring. After all, I thought, if one year of treatment reduces a patient's risk of reoccurrence by 46 percent, shouldn't two years of treatment reduce the chances even more?

The French study said no. It found that one year of treatment seemed to offer the best odds against cancer reoccurrence. Interestingly, though, the study also examined the odds of reoccurrence after only six months of treatment. This part of the study intrigued me since at this point I had already completed over six months of Herceptin treatments. The study found that, after four years, only forty-three out of 3,480 patients that had been treated with Herceptin for only six months had a reoccurrence of cancer.[8] That's only 1 percent. *So, you mean to tell me I'm putting myself through hell with these Herceptin treatments for only a 1 percent chance of improvement?!* I was *so* willing to take the risk. After all, we are not guaranteed *anything*. I could be hit by a bus tomorrow. And since I was convinced that the Herceptin was causing my anemia, I was ready to discontinue the drug. I wasn't giving up. I just wasn't sure that the path I was on was the correct one since my body seemed to be falling apart.

In the meantime, as I pondered my research and bounced my findings off anyone who would listen, my incision opened up—again.

So back I went to the plastic surgeon's office. I have to hand it to Doctor G and his assistant, Nurse R. They did their best to glue and stitch me together again.

Unfortunately, though, the skin at the incision site was too thin to support the stitches. The next day, the suture holes expanded and started to leak like cut dough. Yet again, Nurse R super-glued me like a child's art project, and we all hoped and prayed it would hold. Doctor G and I discussed what we should do if it didn't. He thought the best course of action would be to take out the implant to take the pressure and stress off the incision. The skin was simply too thin, we thought—probably from the anemia. There was no healing blood, no oxygen, and no collagen getting to the incision site. It was like trying to suture a blown up balloon. The skin was stretched so far it was making it easy to tear, and the more repairs we were making the more I *would* tear. I was literally falling apart at the seams. It seemed odd that only one of the two incisions had opened up. My left breast was healing fine which, ironically, was the cancerous side. Once again, I was reminded that I wasn't the typical breast cancer reconstruction patient.

I didn't want to lose the implant, and I was trying to be the optimist, but it looked like it was too late to save my boob at this point. The Herceptin, or the anemia—or something—had done too much damage. I wish I had read about the "4 Percent Club" sooner and stopped my Herceptin treatments. Maybe it would have helped my body heal and I could have kept the implant. Maybe.

I finally cried uncle. The implant wasn't going to stay put no matter how much glue and sutures we used. It was time to remove it. Believe it or not, I had a real peace about the decision despite the awkwardness I knew I would feel from being lopsided.

• **Written February 22, 2013, 11:02 A.M.**

Dear Family and Friends,

THANK YOU for your sweet, encouraging words and prayers. Thank you. Wanted to let you all know this transfusion helped, my Hb levels went up to a 9.5, and I feel a lot better. Funny how a 9.5 (which is still low—normal is 12-13 for women), can feel so great after hanging out in the mid 8's for a few months.

Bone marrow biopsy is scheduled March 11. Praying that the mystery is solved before then, but willing to do the test if I have to.

Thanks for your prayers, love, and support.

Love you and praying for you.

- **Written March 1, 2013, 8:16 P.M.: While I'm Waiting**

The other day Joe was singing this, and he said this song is so right on with our situation: "While I'm Waiting" by John Waller.

I had my bone marrow biopsy yesterday. It got moved up since this could be the problem. No news yet, which to me is good news. The pathologist said he would have the report back by Monday, but if he saw any of the bad stuff he would call. No news is good news. I'm very thankful that it probably isn't any of the scary bone marrow stuff, but it puts us back at square one. What is causing the anemia? My numbers dropped back down this week, so the transfusion only lasted about a week.

Last week a small part of my reconstruction incision started to split. The surgeon cut it open, drained it, and put a few stitches in it. They are not sure if the anemia is causing this or if an infection is causing the anemia, so I went on hardcore IV antibiotics. Today, the surgeon had to open the whole incision to drain it and put a drain line back in.

So as we wait, wait to heal, wait to get back to life, and wait to not think about cancer, we will serve our Heavenly

Father. He will always take care of us and He will always provide. We trust that He will completely heal me, and while we wait we will praise Him!

God Bless you and praying for you as you pray for us.

In Jesus' Precious Love,
Kari

- **Written March 4, 2013, 3:21 P.M.: O Praise Him!**

Dear Mighty Prayer Warriors,

I have a few HUGE praises.

Got off the phone with the pathologist, and I have no bone marrow problem. Healthy bone marrow. I can't even begin to tell you what happiness and peace this brings our family. We can put the lid on that can of worms. YAY GOD!

Saw my surgeon today, and the incision is healing well. He put a drain back in me last week and took a culture, but it came back negative: no infection, the cellulitis is gone, and I may get to keep my boob! (I was hoping I didn't have to lose my breast twice in one year!) So this indicates that the anemia caused the incision to come open and to not heal. Things don't work well without oxygen.

Anyway, the anemia problem isn't solved yet, but I truthfully don't care. They'll figure it out, hopefully before all the blood has left my body. I'm just overjoyed I don't have to do any more chemo right now, don't have to do a bone marrow transplant, and don't have to go into isolation, and I can keep my breasts. The next thing to look at for the doctors is my Herceptin IV (the treatments I still get every three weeks). It's not a chemo. It is an immuno-therapy targeted at one of the proteins that caused my cancer to get aggressive. If they have to stop treatment, I've still had ten out of the seventeen, so that is better than nothing. We'll see what happens. I just wanted to update you all on the two bits of wonderful news we got today.

THANK YOU for praying for us, for interceding, for pleading for us. It's working and I love how God is working in all of our lives.

Love you all, God bless you, and PRAISE HIM!

In Jesus' Precious Love,
Kari

- **Written March 8, 2013, 12:04 P.M.: Whom Shall I Fear (God of Angel Armies)**

Dear Faithful Praying Family and Friends,

I want to share with you something. Last night, Rob, our church's worship pastor, introduced this song "Whom I Shall Fear (God of Angel Armies)" by Chris Tomlin. This morn when Holly came over to give me my antibiotic IV, she had just heard the story behind the song and shared it with me. Chris Tomlin explains it well on You Tube. The bottom line is we have God's angel armies surrounding us and protecting us all the time.

Rob and Holly, THANK YOU! I know God is using you all to encourage me. Thank you for your prayers.

So yesterday was good and rough all at the same time. I won't go into the details. God is working in His timing, and I think out of all of this I am learning it really is *His* timing. He is in control no matter what any doctor or medical study says is going to happen. Our time here is only a thin little scratch on the grand timeline. And the POWER of PRAYER (especially in my weakness: 1 Corinthians 12:9) is overwhelmingly awesome.

My numbers went up from a week ago. YAY GOD and PRAISE GOD! There is only one explanation: God. Tuesday, all my numbers had continued to go down, but yesterday my numbers were up. YAY, YAY, YAY.

So, if I haven't exhausted you all for prayer, could I please ask for you to pray for supernatural protection from the Herceptin? The doctor is leaning toward the assumption that the medicine is making me sick and she is willing to lower my dose, but she is not willing to stop the treatment altogether for fear of the cancer coming back. So I am praying and asking for prayer that God would just keep healing me as this is all going on and for protection for the next six months.

Thank you, thank you for your prayers and encouragement and smiles, laughs, jokes (I need some more of those), and love.

I love you all! Thanks for taking care of my family and me.

In Jesus' Precious Love,
Kari—trying to fight like a girl!

Six

TIME FOR A TRIPLE MASTECTOMY

On March 22, Doctor G removed my right implant and replaced it with a deflated skin expander.

Thankfully, the surgery went well. And the best part: I saw Jesus as I was regaining consciousness. He had his right arm around me and his left arm around Joe, and we watched our children play dodgeball. I'm not sure about the significance of the dodgeball game, but perhaps he was telling me, "Kari, I've got you all. I want you to go have some fun over Spring Break." Unlike after the last surgery, I felt his peace and love. I knew I had made the right decision to remove the implant in order for my right side to heal.

Unfortunately, I was now very obviously lopsided. I still had a perfect left breast but was starting over with the reconstruction on my right side. I had officially lost three boobs in one year.

Needless to say, I was demoralized. I kept second guessing my decision to do the double mastectomy in the first place. After all, my right side never had any cancer. Was the tissue on my right side pissed that I cut off a perfectly good boob? It sure seemed like it was taking its own sweet time to heal.

The surgery fell the week before Spring Break. For a long time, the kids and I had been planning to accompany my husband on his yearly business trip to Texas. It had become an annual tradition. We usually spent one night, either at the beginning or end of the trip, at a Great Wolf Lodge, complete with indoor waterpark. Despite the long twelve hour drive, it represented an opportunity to be together as a family, and all of us eagerly looked forward to this road trip. And, believe me, I really needed to get away.

Both Doctor G and the infectious disease doctor, Doctor D, gave me the green light to go. Despite the recent surgery, they both recognized my emotional weariness and agreed that it would be a great idea to get out of town and forget about all of this. I was still giving myself the antibiotic Cubicin via central line, and I had drains and tubes hanging out of me, so it was kind of hard to completely forget my circumstances. But I praise God for giving me this time away with my family—away from doctors' offices and appointments—for a solid week to focus on him in all of my pain.

It was a hard trip. I was in a lot of discomfort because I didn't want to take any of my pain killers in case Joe needed me to drive. I wanted to slip away. I wanted to sit in God's lap and cry. I tried to focus on the verse in Revelation 7:17 that talks about God wiping away every tear we have ever shed when we get to heaven. But I knew I was falling into an emotional pit. The future looked bleak. I started to doubt all my plans: the Florida trip we had planned in a month, the triathlon in August I had planned as a celebration of beating cancer, and my twenty year college reunion in September. I started feeling sorry for myself. I had done *everything* every doctor had asked me to do and still this happened to me. I felt worse, and weaker, than after any of my chemotherapy treatments. Oh boy, was I a mess!

- **Written March 21, 2013, 7:02 P.M.: Surgery #3: Third Mastectomy**

"'Do not be afraid. Stand firm and you will see the deliverance the LORD will bring you today...The LORD will fight for you; you need only to be still'" (Exodus 14:13-14 NIV).

Thank you, family and friends, for all your prayers. It's been a rough last few weeks, and I wanted to update you.

My red blood counts dropped again, and I won another blood transfusion three weeks after the last. My incision came open again. The surgeon said the skin is so paper-thin at the incision site that it is having a hard time healing. So, after several attempts to try to glue me back together, the surgeon thinks the best course of action is to take the implant out, clean it out, put an empty expander back in, and let my incision heal to take the stress and pressure off. We'll see what happens.

So tomorrow morn at 7:15 A.M., I will be under the knife again for my "tri-lateral" mastectomy. I didn't think it was possible to lose three breasts in one year, but I have a huge peace about this now. I've been crying and lamenting all week. I mean, who really wants to be lopsided? Who wants to recover from another surgery? Fortunately, I have had a few friends remind me of this passage:

"Therefore we do not lose heart. Though outwardly we are wasting away, yet inwardly we are being renewed day by day. For our light and momentary troubles are achieving for us an eternal glory that far outweighs them all. So we fix our eyes not on what is seen, but on what is unseen. For what is seen is temporary, but what is unseen is eternal" (2 Corinthians 4:16-18 NIV).

God's word always gives me peace. Praise the Lord!

Thank you for praying for my red blood cell numbers to go up, because they have after the transfusion last week. Hb is 10.5, and Hct 32.6...I haven't seen numbers like this since September. So that makes me a good candidate for the surgery, too. (The surgeon wanted to make sure I was strong and healthy enough before he operated.)

So, thank you again for your prayers. God is answering them and doing miracles in His timing and in His way— and His way is higher than ours, thank God for that.

God bless you and Happy Spring Break! We love you and are very blessed by you. May God bless you abundantly!

In Jesus' Precious Love,
Kari

- **Written March 22, 2013, 6:03 P.M.: Good Surgery**

   "Praise the LORD, O my soul;
   all my inmost being, praise his holy name.
   Praise the LORD, O my soul,
   and forget not all his benefits—
   who forgives all your sins
   and heals all your diseases,
   who redeems your life from the pit
   and crowns you with love and compassion,
   who satisfies your desires with good things
   so that your youth is renewed like the eagle's" (Psalm 103:1-5 NIV).

Hello Dear Prayer Warriors,

Surgery went well. Implant out, flat chested on one side, perfect boob on the other; however, removable padded bra with two or three extra pads makes for a nice rack.

God is good. Jesus was with me the whole time with His arm around me as I nestled my head into His chest and His arm around Joe the whole time as we watched the kids play dodgeball....

Love you all and thanks for praying. Pretty wiped out so resting with the fam.

God Bless you.

In Jesus' Precious Love,
Kari

In bitterness of soul Hannah wept much and prayed to the LORD.

1 Samuel 1:10 NIV

Seven

A DEEP DARK PIT

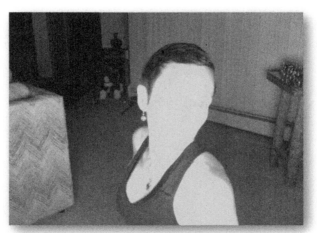

This picture portrays how I was truly feeling: identity-less and washed out.

*I*t was traumatic at first to think about losing my two, God-given boobs to cancer. I had been a member of the "big rack" club all my life, and my boobs were like best friends—my great "supporters." Losing them, I thought, was going to be devastating. I was so wrong. In the beginning, when I first started talking to the surgeon about the reconstruction, I actually got excited. After all, I was going to get a really great rack out of an otherwise lousy deal.

Before my (first) bilateral mastectomy, I had nightmares for weeks about what a deformed, boob-less "me" would look like. I was relieved to find out that I would never be completely flat-chested. During the mastectomy, the surgeon implanted temporary balloons, called skin expanders, and filled them half way with saline. I had beautiful little perfect boobies. I was so happy to have this nice little rack—and no more cancer.

Please don't call me vain. Prior to cancer, I had neither cared nor spent much time on how I looked. But this was going to be different. Thankfully, a few of my closest friends kept reminding me of that verse in Corinthians: *"That is why we never give up. Though our bodies are dying, our spirits are being renewed every day. For our present troubles are small and won't last very long. Yet they produce for us a glory that vastly outweighs them and will last forever! So we don't look at the troubles we can see now; rather we fix our gaze on things that cannot be seen. For the things we see now will soon be gone, but the things we cannot see will last forever"* (2 Corinthians 4:16-18).

This verse comforted me and continues to comfort me to this day. After the first mastectomy, my mental and physical recovery wasn't as bad as I thought. I had a great peace. I give God the credit for that. I felt like he took my focus off my chest and put it all on him so I could begin to prepare for chemo.

Fast forward seven months to our Spring Break vacation. I had just lost my third boob. I was still suffering from severe anemia and no doctor knew why. I couldn't imagine having blood transfusions every three weeks for the next five months. I couldn't imagine worrying about my incisions coming undone again, even with no pressure on them. I felt hopeless. This was a very dark time for me.

Here is a glimpse at my journal from that week, real-time:

<u>March 25</u>: So this is where I'm at today. My implant came out three days ago. (Thank You, Lord, that You gave me a vision of <u>You</u> after my surgery.)

My family and I headed out to Texas for my hubby's business trip and Spring Break. Last night we stayed at the Great Wolf Lodge. I couldn't partake because I still have a healing, open wound, central line, and drain hanging out of my extremely lopsided chest. I'm not quite ready to put on a swimsuit. I got to rest, though, which is what I need after the surgery. So all is good. But, again, I can't tell you how hard it is for this girl to sit on the side lines, especially when I can't be part of life with my family.

<u>March 26</u>: Today at lunch I observed my eleven-year-old look across the table at me with empty eyes, trying to figure out why her mom has been stripped of her outer dignity and beauty, trying to figure out if she should be scared-again-that her mom might not make it. Should she detach and be cold to spare her heart? She was desperately trying to figure it out. I can't stand seeing her eyes searching for these answers. Why does her mom have to look like this, and why does her mom have to feel all this pain, to be so weak, and to look so sick? Why, God, why? Please stop all of this. It's too painful. Please make it all quit. Haven't we endured enough? I know it's not even as much as Your son endured on the cross, but we are weak, sinning humans. Why do my kids have to go through this? What kind of strength are they going to gain from this? And why must my dear husband endure watching my outward body continue to fall apart at the seams? Why are we

stretched so thin financially, too? He's faithfully tithing. Why God? Please make it stop.

I excused myself to go to the bathroom, and the song "Just Breathe" by Anna Nalick was playing. How appropriate. *God, you are always here, always around, and always taking care of me even in the middle of my tantrums.* God said, **"Never will I leave you; never will I forsake you.' So we say with confidence, 'The Lord is my helper; I will not be afraid"** (Hebrews 13:5-6 NIV).

Earlier this morning, I read a devotion from Pastor Ed Dobson. In it, Pastor Dobson emphasizes that he's not afraid of being dead. After all, he knows where he's going. But he's afraid of *getting* dead. Whenever he would sink into despair, he would take a five minute time-out to remind himself of God's promise in Hebrews 13:5-6.[9] I've started this practice, too. It completely helped me emerge from the Steak and Shake restaurant bathroom today in Grapevine, Texas.

The truth is, I'm not sure I'm going to make it through this. *Something* will cause my death, and as of this moment I'm having a difficult time seeing past this cancer. But, like Pastor Dobson, I'm not afraid of death. I know where I'm going. **"If you confess with your mouth that Jesus is Lord and believe in your heart that God raised him from the dead, you will be saved. For it is by believing in your heart that you are made right with God, and**

it is by confessing with your mouth that you are saved" (Romans 10:9-10).

<u>March 28</u>: Another one of those moments I just want to die. This is what a bad day looks like. My husband rejects me from sex. I know it's because he can't stand my deformed chest. It really is grotesque. If it had been a regular mastectomy, I think it would be so much better. But because I had a full implant in it, the skin is stretched out. I'm not sure, but I believe the nipple is sewed on to something to keep it centered, so it is pushed in like a deflated balloon with the nipple hidden under the extra skin like a deflated soufflé. Can you say FREAK?! My oldest daughter is making one of her aunts her new mom. I know she needs someone, but I can't tell you how painful it is to have her look at me like I'm a freak *and* to have her tell some other adult woman how much she loves and misses her. I've already been replaced, and I'm not even dead yet.

Choose life. Choose life. Choose life. Reject the lies!

<u>March 29</u>: Another divine encounter at dinner. We are still on Spring Break. We left Dallas yesterday to hook up with some friends that are stationed in Altus, Oklahoma. Great lunch break to see them. Anyway, we make it to Amarillo. We always stay at the same place because we usually have enough points to get a free night. Plus, they have breakfast and dinner. Anyway, the dinner hostess has been the same sweet lady for

at least the last four years, and she recognized us, as we did her. Usually, it's a casual "hello," or "wow, the kids are getting bigger," but tonight she noticed my lack of hair and my central line. I could see the questions formulating in her eyes before she even asked, "I know you, but you look different." She continued, "It's good to see you again. I like your haircut." I wanted to tell her this was the result of chemo, but I was exhausted, not in a good mood, and was convinced my husband and oldest daughter were done with me.

Then out of the blue, she starts telling me about her grandchildren. And she specifically says, "I recognize you, but your hair is a lot shorter." I tell her I'm fighting breast cancer. She says, "I knew it. I see that thing on your chest, a port, and I knew it. I'm so sorry." She proceeds to tell me about her oldest granddaughter who was recently diagnosed with liver cancer. She is only twenty-two and has a three-year-old and a three-month-old. *Okay, Kari, stop feeling sorry for yourself!* I let the hostess just talk and talk, and then I do something that I don't normally do in the middle of a restaurant with strangers. I pray out loud for her and her granddaughter. I like to pray. I am blessed to be one of the prayer leaders at our church. I sometimes pray spontaneously, but it is usually with people I know. I don't know where this courage came from. Oh, yes I do. THANK YOU LORD!

She gave me her address and phone number. She wanted me to stay in touch, and she wanted me to pray and encourage her granddaughter. O Lord, are you sure? I'm not even through my own fire, and you want me to "cheerlead" someone else? Only with You are all things possible.

<u>March 30</u>:   Tired. Tired again. As much as I want the hemoglobin and hematocrit numbers to stay high and keep getting higher, I want something to justify why I could take a nap in the middle of downtown Amarillo. Maybe it's the painkillers? That could be, but I have only allowed myself to take them at night after we are settled just in case my husband needed me to drive, or we run out of gas and have to split up. (Thank You, Lord that this didn't happen. We came close during the first part of this trip, but you helped us coast in on fumes!)

Will find out Monday my lab results. We'll see if I've dropped from my surgery. I really don't want a drop. I want to go up, let's say to a 16. That would be great, but I want to *feel* like a 16, too. Sometimes I wonder if I'll ever be able to shake this "co-dependence" on sickness. For the last five months, I've been really sick. That seems to be my identity. I know it's only been five months, and I am thankful that it hasn't been years. Will I even be able to identify what feeling good looks and feels like? Yes, the last two blood transfusions have helped me feel good. Within a day of the transfusions, I've felt like living and not sleeping in my bed all day. I was really up from my surgery. Thank

You, Jesus that my hemoglobin was up to a 10.5, the highest it has been in six months.

I'm almost done with the heavy pain killers. Last surgery I tore up the prescription since it was supposed to be a walk in the park. I remember the surgeon saying I could return to work the next day and that I could take Motrin for the pain. So I was really surprised I got a prescription for oxycodone. I hate having stuff like this in the house, especially since they said I wouldn't need it. So I decided to shred the prescription. Stupid! Stupid! I think *any* surgery, if the doctor gives you pain killers, you should take them-especially a surgery where they separate your pectoral muscles to put an implant in. My whole chest was so sore. But I kept telling myself, "This is the easy surgery." So I just took Motrin. Stupid.

This time I'm taking my oxycodone. Only at night, though, for this week. The doctor gave me Celebrex, too. Love that one. Not a narcotic, doesn't make me loopy, and I feel like I can engage with the world. When I take oxycodone-forget it-the world is moving too fast. I just retreat to my happy place. I understand how people can develop addictions to pain meds. They take all the pain away, not only the physical but also the emotional. Comfortably numb.

So maybe, and hopefully, this is why I'm tired. Although if my hemoglobin and hematocrit numbers are up in a couple of days, it will be very hard to debate/fight with my onco to take a break or stop Herceptin.

Yesterday while driving from Dallas to Altus, we heard on the news that scientists are close to a cure for cancer. A protein on cancer cells tricks our immune system into thinking the cancer cells are supposed to be there, causing them to grow and become tumors. The scientists are working on a drug that targets the protein to shut it down. They've had 100% success in mice. This reminded me of why I'm taking Herceptin. It is an immune therapy targeted at the HER2 protein. We all have it on our cells. My cells, however, started developing more and more HER2, and the HER2 protein told my immune system, "We're friendlies. We are *supposed* to be here." And my immune system said, "Okay. Let us know if you need anything." And voila! A whole breast full of cancer. I wonder how this starts. Three months earlier, clean breasts. What happened in those three months? I don't know if I'll ever know, but it's just another reminder that cancer can get anyone. No one is exempt.

So back to this news report. I think that is great! I wonder how long it will take to get this drug out on the market. It sounds like a "super" Herceptin. But instead of targeting just HER2 proteins, it will be smart and target any of those proteins that tell our immune system that cancer cells are on our side. Funny, I always thought I had a good, tough, immune system. I never imagined it would betray me like this.

As you can tell, I had a lot on my mind. I was still debating my doctor's orders to stay with the Herceptin treatments. I kept thinking, "What if God wants me to keep taking it? What if his will is entirely different than what I think? What if he is using me to help the doctors since they have never seen a patient react to Herceptin this way?" I knew his healing power could rescue me from death. I've read the story of Lazarus being brought back to life in the Bible and, of course, Jesus himself rising from the dead. But at that moment, I really felt like I was dying.

Eight

MAD COW DISEASE: GOOD NEWS IN THE BACTERIUM?

On April 1, I received the biggest surprise of my life. Apparently, the culture the doctor took when he removed my implant nine days earlier grew *mycobacterium Senegalense,* an extremely rare bacterium found mostly in African cattle. *Are you kidding me? African cattle?* My friends started teasing that I had contracted Mad Cow Disease! They were right—I was certainly going mad.

Google *mycobacterium Senegalense* and only a handful of hits come up. In fact, it's so rare that there have been only a few case studies on it (although maybe now *my* name comes up!). My infectious disease doctor, Doctor D, surmised that the bacterium had somehow attached itself to the implant during manufacture and then began multiplying inside my body after surgery. But I could tell he really had no clue where it came from. My plastic surgeon's sentiments were the same. How and why did such a rare bacterium end up in *my* body? It will for sure be a question I ask God when I come into his holy presence!

At any rate, the presence of the bacterium, along with my nagging anemia, was clearly hindering my surgical recovery and may have been a major contributing factor to my incision opening up. Doctor D told me to think of it as "pond scum" that, although stagnant, was producing enough fluid at the incision site to prevent it from healing. Yuck!

I couldn't help but to think that all this had been a cruel April Fool's joke. I had never been to Africa, and I certainly hadn't been playing around with any cows, but now I suddenly had a "mad cow pond scum" inside of me. I was speechless. God knew all of this was going to happen. He didn't cause it, but he was allowing me to go through it. But why? Did the world hate me? I felt bombarded.

All I could do was repeat that verse over and over again: *"[Christ's] power is made perfect in [my] weakness"* and *"[His] grace is sufficient for [me]"* (2 Corinthians 12:9 NIV).

Doctor D consulted the infectious disease specialists at Jewish National Hospital in Denver, and we came up with a new plan of attack: switch to heavier-hitting antibiotics, leave the skin expander in for now without filling it with saline, and wait. We would wait and pray that the new antibiotics would kill whatever was inside me. We would wait and pray that I would start to heal. Admittedly, my entire treatment plan was a crap shoot based on only two other known cases of this bacterium in humans. But it was the best we had to go on.

- **Written April 1, 2013, 3:20 P.M.: Wait For It**

   This morning I was reminded of one of God's many promises, a promise that God *will* provide but sometimes maybe not until the last minute:

   "'God himself will provide the lamb for the burnt offering, my son'" (Genesis 22:8 NIV).

   This verse refers to the story of Abraham being told by God to sacrifice his son Isaac—the son he loved and waited so long for. At the last moment, when Abraham was about to kill his son, God stopped him and provided a lamb.

This story holds a powerful lesson. As we make our way up the mountain of struggles, God is ALREADY coming up on the other side with a lamb. At the right time, we will meet at the summit.

We need His grace. It's all we need. It's sufficient for all our needs.

"'My grace is all you need,
My power works best in weakness'" (2 Corinthians 12:9).

The above verse gives me lots of peace. I know God is going to let me know what to do in regard to my upcoming treatment. It just might be at the last moment. Wait for it. Wait for it!

This morning I met with the infectious disease doctor and plastic surgeon. My body somehow was infected with *mycobacterium Senegalense*. If you Google it you won't find much info on it—that is how rare it is. Both doctors couldn't believe that this was real. The few reported cases of this develop in Africa in cattle, so for humans to develop this is very rare. There is some case of a human developing this due to a catheter-associated infection. She was apparently the first case for humans. I don't know how long ago that was. The GREAT thing is that this is what caused my incision to keep opening, to leak, and to not heal—not the Herceptin and not my body rejecting the implant. The other GREAT thing is that *mycobacterium Senegalense* doesn't infect the whole body. It is contained in a little pocket. So the next course of action is to find out if it is still in my body and, if so, to treat it.

Another PRAISE, and yes, I call all of the above a praise, is that my hemoglobin went up. This is the first time my own body did this since chemo. Healing is happening! PRAISE YOU LORD JESUS! I am still anemic, but the fact that my own body is trying so hard to heal is such a positive sign.

Tomorrow I have another Herceptin scheduled. I am not sure what I am going to do. There is still no answer to what caused the anemia. Lucky me, I have developed two rare things that don't appear to be related, and most doctors haven't seen it before. All I can say is that God knows what He is doing, and if I can be used for His glory, I'm ALL IN!

I apologize if I haven't returned calls, e-mails, and texts. The last five weeks have had me going to three different specialists nearly every day. I'm kind of behind on my correspondence, but I appreciate your prayers and your thoughts. It's still a long road ahead, but I feel like today was such a huge breakthrough with finding answers. Even though I have some weird and rare things going on in my body, I have a family that loves and takes such great care of me, friends that have helped out in so many ways that I will never be able to say thank you appropriately, a team of medical doctors and nurses dedicated to helping me, a great and MIGHTY prayer support team, and a God that is the ultimate healer.

Much love. God Bless you.

In Jesus' Precious Love,
Kari

- **Written April 2, 2013, 5:08 P.M.: #12 Done!**

Twelfth Herceptin done!

I am trusting God to supernaturally protect my body, which I know He will. His answer was pretty clear in what I should do, so who can refute God? I mean, I know I refute Him all the time in little daily decisions—every time I worry, or get anxious, or fail to have patience, and in many more ways. I'm a sinner, plain and simple. I am SOOOOOOOOOO glad that God sent us Jesus to die for our sins and to give us righteousness through Jesus, so we could have eternal life.

Prayer warriors, thank you for speaking the name of Jesus into this. I totally can see His perfect power in my weakness. Thank you.

We are still awaiting the course of action with the antibiotics. It will probably be several months of treatment with three antibiotics in the hopes that two of them actually work and don't build a resistance. So I guess another prayer request: pray that the antibiotics work and I don't build a resistance to them. Then, they can begin to think about the reconstruction. Until then, I will be uni-boob. Maybe I will get a new boob for next Christmas! Don't worry—I won't re-gift last year's Christmas present boob.

Thank you, thank you, and thank you for all your prayers. Please let me know how I can specifically pray for you. I am praying for you, but I would love to pray specifically for you.

Happy spring! God bless you, and love you.

In Jesus' Precious Love,
Kari

Nine

A New Attitude—Again!

*Is there any encouragement from belonging to
Christ? Any comfort from his love? Any fellowship
together in the Spirit? Are your hearts tender and
compassionate? Then make me truly happy by agreeing
wholeheartedly with each other, loving one another,
and working together with one mind and purpose.*

Philippians 2:1-2

$\mathcal{Y}$es, I badly wanted these promises to be true in my life, but there's more verses:

*"Don't be selfish; don't try to impress others. Be humble,
thinking of others as better than yourselves. Don't look out
only for your own interests, but take an interest in others, too"*

(Philippians 2:3-4).

I really struggled here. At this point in my treatment, cancer was *supposed* to be behind me. My chest should have been completely reconstructed by now, and I should have been getting healthier and stronger every day. People would ask me, in so many words, "What's your problem? The chemo is done, and you're supposed to be getting back to normal and on with your life." Yes, I really had people say things like that to me. Certainly, I have put my foot in my mouth before, but God really had to show me how to extend his grace to people who made comments like that in moments of complete stupidity.

Believe me, I wanted to be better. I was sick of Herceptin and sick of being anemic. I hated starting over again with my breast reconstruction, at least on the one side, and I hated not knowing if the antibiotics were working to kill the bacterium. Our finances were being exhausted, and it seemed like there was no end in sight to my illness, no light at the end of the tunnel, and no timetable for feeling "normal."

Then it hit me. I will *never* be the same again, nor do I want to be. My life will forever be defined by a new normal. But what do I do while it plays out? What do I do while I wait? I decided I would do my best to serve God, to praise him, and to thank him!

Though he was God,
he did not think of equality with God
as something to cling to.
Instead,
he gave up his divine privileges;
he took the humble position
of a slave
and was born as a human being.
When he appeared in
human form,
he humbled himself
in obedience to God
and died a criminal's death
on a cross.
Therefore, God elevated him
to the place of highest honor
and gave him the name above all other names,
that at the name of Jesus
every knee should bow,
in heaven and on earth and under the earth,
and every tongue confess that Jesus Christ is Lord,
to the glory of God the Father

PHILIPPIANS 2:6-11

Ten

WHILE I'M WAITING

I was locked in a game of wait-and-see. I had to wait to see if my incision would heal. I had to wait to see if the antibiotics would kill the bacterium. I had to wait to see if the reduced dosages of Herceptin would allow my red blood cells to recover. I had to wait to look normal since the unfilled tissue expander on my right side made me look lopsided. And the wait was, at times, agonizing.

Even with my family and friends constantly reminding me to hold every thought captive to God, it was still difficult to keep from imagining the myriad of worst-case scenarios. Since I was finally feeling decent, I decided to jump into some volunteer work to keep my mind occupied. I kept score for our son's Little League team and volunteered for some administrative work at our kids' school. During chemo I had stayed away from the school as much as possible for two reasons: (1) germs—most of my chemo was during flu season; and (2) I was so afraid I would scare the little kids since I had no eyebrows or eye lashes!

Both volunteer jobs blessed me since they kept me from thinking about whether or not the bacterium was still growing. Even though I felt exhausted at the end of each event, I kept reminding myself that Jesus came to serve, not to be served. He suffered and endured more than I'll ever experience. I thought, if Jesus could serve others even as he was being tortured to death, I certainly could serve others while I was waiting.

Having this mindset helped prevent me from falling back into the emotional pit. Life didn't stop just because I was sick. My husband had to go to work. I wanted my children to continue with their activities. We would continue to experience the normal curveballs thrown at every family—like blizzards, for instance.

Blizzard warnings don't scare us in Colorado, even in April. But what did scare me was our furnace going out the night before a huge cold and biting storm. Of course, my husband was out of town! But, as usual God provided for us.

I had been reading *Upside-Down Prayers for Parents* by Lisa T. Bergren. In it she says:

> The things in life that come easily are rarely the things that bring us fulfillment and joy. Superficial relationships. Stuff that money can buy. Activities that fill our days but don't make life fulfilling. These aren't the things that we'll value over time or remember as turning points, defining events that shaped our lives.[10]

I will definitely remember that blizzard. The kids and I had to work together to bring in wood and to tend the fires in the stoves to keep the house warm enough to prevent our thirty-year-old pipes from freezing. In the meantime, we made the most of it by snuggling to keep warm, making hot chocolate, popping corn, and watching movies. Every breath is a gift.

Anyway, our April blizzard was just another reminder that spring is an oxymoron in Colorado. We'll have a few nice days in April and May interspersed with wet, heavy periods of snow that melts as quickly as it comes. It's a good time to take a vacation, and for many years we had jetted off to meet my husband Joe's family on Sanibel Island, Florida, for some warmth and sunshine. Since I was feeling decent, we decided to continue the tradition this year.

A few days before we were supposed to leave, the specialists at Jewish National Hospital in Denver contacted my own doctors and advised them that their latest recommendation for treating the bacterium was to take the tissue expander out and to continue treating me with three new antibiotics. In essence, they wanted my plastic surgeon to start over—again!

I love my doctors! Both my infectious disease doctor, Doctor D, and my plastic surgeon, Doctor G, realized enough was enough. They knew I had been to hell and back with this reconstruction. Since my body was showing no signs that the bacterium was still present, they decided to go against the recommendations of the specialists. Collectively, we decided to leave the expander in and continue treating with the antibiotics I was already on. They were both hopeful (even the notoriously pessimistic infectious disease doctor) that the bacterium had been removed with the implant. Hooray! I could go to Florida!

Sanibel Island was a great escape, and we had the best condo on the beach, but it was very hard to be there. I was still lopsided. I was still unable to do anything but walk. I was still trying to force a smile and pretend all was good. I was still struggling to be still.

Fortunately, my family didn't hold any of that against me. For the most part, they let me rest, cry, and be a hermit. My sister-in-law gave me the idea to "forgive" the bacterium. When you hold a grudge against someone, or some*thing*, it prevents *you* from healing and moving on. I desperately wanted to move on. So I forgave *mycobacterium Senegalense* for interrupting my healing.

About the time we returned from Florida, Doctor D allowed me to discontinue all the antibiotics I had been on. For eleven weeks, I had been on various combinations of antibiotics since none of the experts were sure which drug would be the most effective against the bacterium. I was starting to feel sick from this latest combination of Doxycycline, Ciprofloxacin, and Clarithromycin—three heavy-hitting antibiotics.

Plus, my ever-observant pharmacist reminded us all that the combination of Cipro and Clarithromycin could cause heart damage over time. (Perhaps my dad, who was a pharmacist himself, was protecting me from heaven.) Doctor D and I agreed that if the most powerful antibiotics known to man hadn't killed the bacterium in eleven weeks, then nothing would. Anyway, since I had forgiven the bacterium and given it permission to leave my body, I knew deep down inside that it was gone.

Me and my J resting in Sanibel.

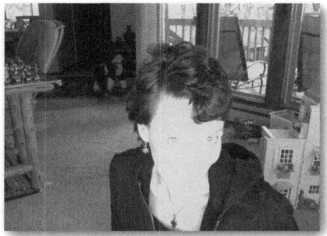

"Hair! It's growing!"

- **Written May 7, 2013, 6:30 P.M.: Learning to Surrender**

Hello Family and Friends.

Thank you for your continued prayers for my fam and me. This has certainly been an endurance road that God is using to teach me so many things.

Joe and I and some friends from our church had the chance to worship with Chris Tomlin, Kari Jobe, and Louie Giglio at Red Rocks this last weekend. For me, this was the concert of a lifetime—like I had died and gone to heaven! It was definitely what I needed to stay encouraged and to inspire me in my relationship with Jesus.

Joe's cousin shares excerpts from the book *Jesus Calling* with all of her husband's CaringBridge entries. I want to share from this morning's devotion, since this is something I am still really working on in my own life. I hope it motivates you as it does me. Read as if Jesus were talking to you:

> If you learn to trust Me—really trust Me—with your whole being, then nothing can separate you from My Peace. Everything you endure can be put to good use by allowing it to train you in trusting Me....
>
> ...Relax in My sovereignty, remembering that I go before you, as well as with you, into each day. *Fear no evil*, for I can bring good out of every situation you will ever encounter.[11]

So as we wait in the midst of my treatments, reconstructions, surgeries, etc., Jesus is teaching me how to truly and totally surrender to Him. I have a long way to go in learning this. I am praying for you and your family and hope things are well and you are seeing all the "love notes" God is leaving you.

Check out Chris Tomlin's song, "God's Great Dance Floor." He played it to open up and to close the concert. I'm still jumping up and down to this.

In Jesus' Precious Love,
Kari

P.S. Still doing Herceptin. Number fourteen next week. Still working on the whole mycobacterium situation, too. Doctors aren't sure if it's still in me, so they are pressing forward in my healing as if it has left my body. If it's still in me, it will rear its ugly head in the next few weeks, and then I will go back to the starting line—again. Even though this has been frustrating and discouraging, God has me keenly aware of His presence whether or not I want to recognize it, and He continues to give me the strength and courage to "fight like a girl!"

- **Written June 5, 2013, 12:08 P.M.: Herceptin #15 DONE**!

"Show me the right path, O LORD;
point out the road for me to follow.
Lead me by your truth and teach me,
for you are the God who saves me.
All day long I put my hope in you" (Psalm 25:4-5).

I can't say that following the path the Lord has laid out for me has been easy, especially these last twelve months. But I *can* truly say that there is nothing that will separate me from His great love and never will He leave us or forsake us.

Had my fifteenth treatment yesterday. Only three left with the last one scheduled August 6 at 1 P.M. Then I will be done with all the cancer treatments, hopefully for the rest of my life. Thank you, Father!

Tomorrow marks my anniversary as a one year cancer survivor. Finally, I'm actually starting to feel like a survivor. A couple months ago—not so much! I'm still living with some of the lasting effects of the chemo/cancer treatment, but Jesus has pulled us through the worst of this storm. Thank you, Father!

So what about the mysterious *mycobacterium Senegalense*? Who knows? We are all thinking positive and acting like it's gone from my body, and thanking Jesus for giving us peace about it. My sis-in-love, Lori, taught me how to forgive it, love it, and start living life again. Thanks, Lori!

My surgeon gave me the go ahead to start training for the triathlon I missed last summer due to the mastectomy. It's in twelve weeks. At this point I can't even do one of the events, but I know that ***"I can do all this through him who gives me strength"*** (Philippians 4:13 NIV Biblegateway).

It may not be pretty. I may have to crawl across the finish line. But, with God's grace and strength, I hope to finish it.

I am thankful for God's grace in everything, even the really bad things I struggle with. He is faithful and has given me so much of His perfect grace.

My amazing Joe and our kiddos continually bless me. Thank you for lifting them up in prayer, too.

God bless you! Praying for you as you pray for us! I'm thanking our Heavenly Father for your friendship and love, and for continuing to support us on this path that God has laid out for us.

Love you.

In Jesus' Precious Love,
Kari

Eleven

CHECK ENGINE LIGHT

*N*ow that I was off antibiotics and the doctors were relatively sure that the bacterium was gone, it was time to get my right boob back. Doctor G began the gradual process of refilling the tissue expander with saline to prepare the skin for a new implant. Since the process would take a few months, I decided I needed something fun to take my mind off of everything. I decided to train for the Iron Girl Triathlon in Denver.

Once again, I was having a hard time sitting around and waiting. My mentor and two-time breast cancer survivor from church would call me Simba, referring to the character in Disney's *Lion King* who just couldn't wait to be king. Actually, it was more like I just couldn't wait to be with *the* king, my heavenly father!

I trained and trained hard. I started in really bad shape, barely able to do any one of the triathlon events, let alone all three in the same workout. The anemia had really taken its toll on my body. I felt weak and got winded easily.

Beginning with my twelfth Herceptin treatment in April, I had been getting lower dosages of the drug. As you recall, I finally convinced my oncologist that the Herceptin was causing my anemia, and my theory was proving correct. Although I was still officially anemic, the lower doses of Herceptin seemed to be allowing my body's hemoglobin to climb. It never again went low enough to trigger another blood transfusion. On August 6, I had my last Herceptin treatment. I had, by the grace of God, completed the entire regimen of seventeen treatments.

All the while, I continued to train for the triathlon, and my endurance slowly started to improve.

It was about this time that the wife of a former colleague reached out to me. Malia, herself an Ironman finisher, contacted me through Facebook and asked if she could train with me, support me, and cheer me on. I felt humbled and honored by her sincerity, especially since we had never met in person. Her husband Derek allowed me to use his super-fast, professional road bike for the cycling portion of the race, thereby saving me the embarrassment of riding my own clunky mountain bike with the child seat attached! I will be forever grateful to the two of them for being my personal cheerleaders.

I felt great on race day. I remember praising God as I got out of the water after the 800 meter swim. *Let me keep going!* I praised and sang to him all twelve miles of the bike ride. I remember telling him while I was pedaling, "No matter what happens with this next surgery, this little party will help me get through it." I praised and thanked him all the way on the five kilometer run, too.

Malia and I finished the race together, although I'm sure it felt more like training to her. She easily caught up to me on the bike and stayed with me for the rest of the race—just to encourage me. Thanks, Malia! For me, it was such a great rush to finish. I truly believe God wanted me to just have fun that day, and I did. All glory and praise to him, because there is no way I could have done it on my own.

I loved what God allowed me to do while we waited that summer. (See the pictures in Appendix 2). Thankfully, my incision continued to heal the whole time. No stitches popping, no draining, no leaking—no nothing. Praise God!

Everything was going so well that Doctor G wanted to "re-install" my right implant in August. By now, he had completely filled the tissue expander and my now-healed incision was tolerating the expansion. He was anxious to swap out the expander with the permanent implant, but he also wanted to honor all the hard work I had been doing to train. I convinced him to postpone the surgery until after Colorado Springs' Race for the Cure in early September, another event we had participated in as a family since 1999. Also, my husband and I had our fourteenth wedding anniversary and twentieth year reunion from the U.S. Air Force Academy to attend over Labor Day weekend—and I certainly wanted to show off my *half* boob job to all my former academy classmates! Ha!

Although the reunion and the race were welcome respites from the drudgery of waiting, I nonetheless felt lost. After the triathlon in August, I started to feel anxious and depressed. I started getting unexplainable headaches. I felt identity-less, even though I knew I was a ***"[child] of God through faith in Christ Jesus"*** (Galatians 3:26). I felt lazy and unproductive and really just longed to have another "mission" from God. I reflected on how I hadn't been a good daughter to my widowed mom and how I hadn't been a good sister to my brother and his wife who were facing life changing decisions of their own. I felt like I was struggling to be a good mom with my own kids and a good wife and partner to my husband. I wasn't holding any thought captive to God; instead, I was allowing Satan to make me believe I was worthless.

For a time, I actually thought that it would be okay if I died during the surgery. After all, I would finally get to come into Jesus' presence. It wasn't that I wanted to give up. I was just tired. I was allowing that sneaky thief, Satan, to put me in another pit of hopeless despair!

Fortunately, Jesus Christ's power was stronger than all of this. I realized I was starting to slide back into the pit. I knew this was not the way God wants us to act. I knew I wasn't glorifying him by acting this way, and I started to hold those thoughts captive. We have ***"divine power to demolish strong holds. We demolish arguments and every pretension that sets itself*** *up against the knowledge of God, and we take captive every thought to make it obedient to Christ"* (2 Corinthians 10:4-5 NIV).

The night before my surgery, the message at church was about anxiousness. *Oh, Father God, I love your timing!* It was a great way to get ready for what I hoped would be my final surgery.

Team Ward at the
Race for the Cure 2013

Team "Kare" Bear

• **Written July 5, 2013: Check Engine Light**

This was the light that illuminated the other day after I stopped to fuel up my car. Since it unexpectedly came on with a couple of other lights, and since it took a couple of turns of the ignition to get the car started (and I knew my fuel cap was on tight), I panicked! I definitely got that "oh-no-the-bottom's-going-to-fall-out-AGAIN!" feeling. It's been a challenging year to say the least. Cancer, enough surgeries to get a frequent punch card, treatments, chemo, complete hair loss, reconstruction problems, medical bills, rare bacteriums, and an extreme unexplainable anemia are just a few of the major things my family and I have faced in the last year, so please forgive me if my reaction to the situation was panic. But our God is good—ALWAYS!

In fact, He reminded me of a verse that very day the car was being difficult: ***"Having hope will give you courage"*** (Job 11:18).

How simple and easy this advice is. Have hope. Choose to believe that the bottom is *not* going to fall out. ***"Do not be anxious about anything, but in everything, by prayers and petition, with thanksgiving, present your requests to God. And the peace of God, which transcends all understanding, will guard your hearts and your minds in Christ Jesus"*** (Philippians 4:6-7 NIV). Have hope. Gain courage. Choosing to look at the good, not the bad, can *and will* give us courage.

Thinking about those lights—the car has seemingly been fine, but the check engine light is still illuminated. When's the last time I checked *my* engine—my heart and my mind? And have I serviced it with God lately?

This morning in *Jesus Calling*, God says to us: "Draw near to Me with a thankful heart…I long to make your life a glorious adventure, but you must stop clinging to old ways."[12]

After reading this and the verses that are referenced to write this devotion, I am confidently reminded that we need to continually check our "engine" and service it with God. He is only a whisper of His Name away.

- **Written August 6, 2013, 10:18 A.M.: Last Herceptin DONE—I SURVIVED!!**

"Even though the fig trees have no blossoms, and there are no grapes on the vines;

**even though the olive crop fails,
and the fields lie empty and barren;
even though the flocks die in the fields,
and the cattle barns are empty,
yet I will rejoice in the LORD!
I will be joyful in the God of my salvation!
The Sovereign LORD is my strength!
He makes me as surefooted as a deer,
able to tread upon the heights"** (Habakkuk 3:17-19).

AMEN and Hallelujah! This battle is finally over. THANK YOU, JESUS!

The last fourteen months I have gotten the sh*# kicked out of me (literally at times), but through Jesus' strength and perfect power, He has allowed me to "fight like a girl" and survive. Thank you, Jesus!

Dear Father, may the scars that are left on my body from this fight always remind me that **"I can do <u>everything</u> through <u>Christ</u> who gives me strength"** *(Philippians 4:13, emphasis added). Thank you, Jesus! Also, may they remind me that there is NOTHING that can separate me from Your love—NOTHING (Romans 8:38-39). Father, let this experience humble me and remind me that there are far worse battles out there than mine, especially the suffering You had to go through just to save a sinner like me. Oh, thank You, Jesus!*

Thank you to all who walked, crawled, and sat on this road with us. There will never be a "thank you" adequate enough! My prayer through all of this is that your relationship with Christ has been deepened as you were selflessly praying for us and helping support us and watching God do miracles all around us. I pray that God has been glorified and praised, and I continue to pray that you will know how much He loves you.

J, you are my hero. You never gave up on me. Even in the darkest, most hopeless days you still believed that God would heal me. You inspired me to hope again. Thank you for all your love and encouragement and for never once rushing me through this journey, but instead allowing God's perfect and sweet timing to carry us through. I love and respect you. Thank you for picking up all the additional work for Team Ward!

Kiddos, you are my little prayer warriors and heroes. I am sorry you had to see this battle up front and personal, but I am so thankful for what God is doing in you right now. Keep your eyes focused on Him, and "oh, no, never let go!" He will never let go of you.

Thank you, Heavenly Father. Thank you, Jesus. Thank you, Holy Spirit.

I am humbled and awed at the triple power that I have been honored to see. Every breath is a gift. I am learning through this journey that "every breath's a battle between drudgery and gratitude and we must keep thanks on the lips so we can sip from the holy grail of joy."[13]

"I feel alive. I come alive. I am alive on God's great dance floor!" (Chris Tomlin, "God's Great Dance Floor," *Burning Lights, sixsteps Records, 2013, CD.*)

Twelve

My Triple Mastectomy—Let's Try This Again

*S*eptember 9, 2013. Plastic surgery to get my right boob back. Again. I was ready for whatever happened. If God didn't want me to wake up after the surgery but instead wanted me to go be in the presence of Jesus—well, that would be great! If God's will for me was to wake up and continue to heal and glorify him—that would be great! If God's will for me was to wake up and to *not* heal and glorify him—that would be pretty lousy…umm, I mean, great, too.

I was really nervous that Monday morning and extremely hungry. I couldn't wait to eat a cheeseburger. Funny, I'm usually never hungry in the morning, but I was famished on the day I couldn't eat. Doesn't that just figure?

My husband, Joe, took me to the surgery center early, and we had a few minutes alone before Pastor Mike and his wife (my best friend) Holly showed up. I barely got to say hello to them before the nurses whisked me back to pre-op.

As I sat alone in my room, I thought about how maybe I hadn't prepared my kids for this surgery. The night before when we were putting them to bed, our four-year-old asked why I was going to be gone in the morning when she woke up. I thought I had already talked about this, but I told her that I was going to have surgery to "put my boobie back."

She said, "Like Hero's Duty?" (We had just watched the movie *Wreck It Ralph.*)

"No, not Hero's Duty, Mommy's boobie." We both giggled. I tucked her in and said good night to all the kids.

A few minutes later, she came out of her room and asked if I would "gingle" (our word for snuggle). I told her no since it was late, and I was tired. I really just wanted to go to bed.

A couple more minutes elapsed. Joe came and asked if I *would* go snuggle with her. She had confided in him that she was afraid of me having surgery. She was afraid the cancer had returned. Wow! After hearing this, I went back to snuggle. I can't believe I didn't better explain the purpose of the surgery. I returned to say good night to all the kids again. I wanted to reassure them that the cancer wasn't back, and that this was a very small surgery to put my boob back. I hugged and kissed them all. It didn't take any of them very long to fall asleep since they had run three miles in the Race for the Cure earlier in the day.

So back to pre-op. Once I was all prepped and ready, Joe, Holly, Mike, and Donna (my worship pastor's wife and a good friend) came back to see me until "go time." They prayed for me, and then we just hung out. Doctor G was running a little behind because of a facelift surgery. I was actually glad that the room was filled with friends to help take our minds off the pending surgery. I'd be lying if I said I wasn't nervous, scared, and frightened. After all, my experiences in the operating room hadn't been good up to that point.

Finally, it was time. I remember saying hi to Nurse R and lying down. I remember the anesthesiologist asking me if I had a heart condition. I remember hearing a weird, arrhythmic beat coming from my heart monitor and thinking, "Well, with all my poor heart has been through in the last year, who could blame its strange beat." Herceptin is very hard on the heart, which is why the physicians monitored it every quarter with an echocardiogram. Who knows, all the antibiotics may have screwed up my heartbeat, too.

Hearing my odd heartbeat made me nervous and anxious. I tried really hard to give every thought back to God, but it was hard not to focus on the strange, tympanic beat. It sounded so weird I almost didn't believe the sound was coming from *my* heart. "When is this anesthesia going to kick in?" I thought. *I feel too awake! Should I shut my eyes? I'll just keep looking around until*—lights out.

I hadn't slept well the night before. Two of our four kids had climbed into bed with us, and neither Joe nor I had the heart to put them back in their own beds. I laid awake most of the night holding them. I was pinned between them, so I couldn't move. I wouldn't have had it any other way, but I was definitely tired because of it.

I remember the recovery nurse, who is also a friend of mine, trying to arouse me after surgery. I felt groggy. I remember looking for Jesus and not seeing him at first. *Oh, no. Not again! Where is Jesus?* Suddenly a peace enveloped me, and I literally felt Jesus' presence squeezing me from all sides as if he were holding me. I couldn't see him, but I felt him holding me. And that was way better. Thank you, Jesus!

I had forgotten how much surgery hurt. During the last one, the surgeon removed the implant which actually took a lot of the stress and pressure off my chest cavity. This time, he added a boob back. Although it was a smaller size implant than the last, the swelling made it appear and feel gargantuan. I was thankful that only one side needed to recover, but I could feel the incision being tugged at with even the slightest movement of my torso.

Thankfully, Doctor G also removed the injection port that had been surgically implanted above my right breast during my very first breast cancer surgery. Hallelujah! I was definitely ready to have that hardware removed after fifteen months. Don't get me wrong. The port facilitated the countless infusions, treatments, and blood draws I had had in the past year by giving the nurses direct access to my vein. Otherwise, I'm sure I would have felt like a human pincushion. But I was still glad to have it removed.

I must have been the office joke the morning of my surgery. Doctor G had once told me that one of his patients forgot to ask him to remove her port and had forgotten to signal her intentions on the consent form. When she awoke from surgery, she started crying because he hadn't taken it out. There was no way I was going to let that happen to me! To make sure, I had taken a sharpie and written on my skin in big bold letters "Plz Remove" with an arrow pointing to my port. I reminded every person who came into the pre-op that I wanted my port removed. I even had Doctor G circle it as he was marking me up for surgery.

But seriously, surgery hurts. This one forced me back to the pain killers. Percocet worked for me. It took away all the pain. However, it also made the world seem too fast. I had a hard time focusing. Just trying to listen to people talk frustrated me.

My husband totally rocks. I was reminded of this again during the weeks following the surgery. He took care of everything. Really, all I had to do was rest. And with this new boob, that is all I wanted to do. No sudden movements. I didn't even want to sneeze I was so afraid I might rip open.

Six days after the surgery, I took my last Percocet and thought, "The party is soon going to be over." The pain that day was still pretty intense, but I held off taking any drugs until I couldn't stand it any longer. *Oh Jesus, please take all this pain away!* I still wasn't certain whether or not all the pain from the reconstruction was worth it. But since I had one nice boob and one not-so-nice, I was kind of stuck. I was either all in or all out at that point.

I also remember thinking that it was time to wrap up this story and get it published. One of my kids, who will forever remain nameless, decided to clean the screen of Daddy's iPhone5 with water. Lots of it. Of course, it seeped into the phone and disabled it. Oh, boy! I don't think I have seen Joe that mad in a long time. That incident, plus a year's worth of out-of-pocket copays and deductibles, made me feel anxious about our finances. I decided I would finish my book so that, if I died tomorrow, Joe could publish it and pocket the money to pay bills.

I knew I was an encourager, and I wanted my book to be encouraging. I also knew that Satan would like nothing more than to take me out to prevent it. I kept reminding myself, "My God is greater. My God is stronger. He is *still* displaying his perfect power in my weakness."

We went to church that night. We showed up at the last minute and ducked out early to avoid the hugging and talking that usually surrounds the service. I was still sore and very much in pain. But as I was sneaking out, I sensed something was wrong. Again.

- **Written September 9, 2013, 11:57 P.M.: Last Surgery**

Hey Family and Friends,

I just wanted to say thank you for your continued prayers, especially on this long journey. I had my (hopefully) last surgery (ever) yesterday. Last winter when I got that strange and rare *mycobacterium senegalense*, it led to the removal of one of my breast implants. Yesterday, I got to get another one put back in. Yay! Hopefully, and Lord willing, this one will be just fine.

I want to just say THANK YOU so much for all the prayers and support in this last year. I am being hopeful and bold, and claiming in the name of Jesus that this is the last cancer related post for me—EVER!!!! Thanks for hanging in there with Team Ward.

Thank you, Prayer Warriors. Much love and appreciation to you!

Happy 14th Anniversary, J. I love you with all my heart!

In Jesus' Precious Love,
Kari

"The Lord is my shepherd; I shall not want.
He makes me lie down in green pastures.
He leads me beside still waters.
He restores my soul.
He leads me in paths of righteousness
for his name's sake.
Even though I walk through the valley of the shadow
of death,
I will fear no evil;
for you are with me;
your rod and your staff,
they comfort me.
You prepare a table before me
in the presence of my enemies;
you anoint my head with oil;
my cup overflows.
Surely goodness and mercy shall follow me
all the days of my life,
and I shall dwell in the house of the LORD
forever" (Psalm 23:1-6 ESV Biblegateway).

Thank you, Jesus!

Thirteen

...AND AGAIN! SURGERY DEBACLE

*A*s I was getting ready for bed that night after church, I noticed my bandages were completely soaked with bright red blood. I freaked. I called the plastic surgeon, Doctor G, apologized for calling him on a Sunday night, and tried to describe the terrifying sight. He talked me down off the ledge and had Joe remove the bandage to be his "eyes." My once beautiful, "no scar" incision was weeping. For the most part, it looked like it was holding together, but fluid was dripping from both ends of the six inch incision. Doctor G instructed us to re-bandage the incision and to come in early the next day. For now, though, he recommended getting some sleep.

Oh, how this road looked all too familiar! Once again, I was really scared.

The next day, we got the kids off to school and headed back to the surgery center. I was pretty sure Doctor G would want to put me under, so I didn't eat or drink anything after we had talked to him the night before. Honestly, I didn't feel like eating anyway. Also, I really didn't want to be awake if he was going to put a drain in me. Back in February when we were trying everything to salvage the first implant, I had lain awake on the table while they put a drain in me. Then, Doctor G and Nurse R did a great job of numbing everything so I didn't feel it, but today I knew I was too much of an emotional wreck to consciously withstand the procedure. "Please put me out," I told them.

When I awoke from this mini-surgery, I was strangely confident that a new drain would fix everything. Not much fluid was coming out, and Doctor G reinforced the incision with additional, and visible, sutures. I didn't care what it looked like as long as I stayed together. I didn't care if I had a scar since only Joe and I would be able to see it. I had long ruled out any strolls down a topless beach! I even thought that having a visible scar would remind us of how God got us through this horrific battle.

I went back to Doctor G's office a few days later. All was well, healing well, and draining well. In fact, he could have taken out the drain, but we both decided to leave it in out of an abundance of caution. We wanted the incision to completely dry up.

The following Sunday night, we returned to church. I actually felt good enough to sing on the Worship Team. All was well. Great worship. Great message. After we got home, though, I noticed that the bulb attached to my drain didn't have any suction. I didn't know if I should be happy or panic. Had I finally hit "sand" in the drain and it was bone dry? Or had the vacuum been destroyed by another unforeseen side effect? I was hopeful that it was the former. Since I wasn't as panicked as the week before, I decided I would wait until morning to call the plastic surgeon's office.

Later that night, the incision started seeping again. We put some Neosporin on it and re-bandaged it, but I knew it wasn't good. My skin was so thin that I could see the blue tubing of the drain underneath. I tried to be hopeful. *Oh, please Lord. Please!*

The next morning, in my quiet time, God comforted me with a verse from Psalms:

> **"Lord, do not rebuke me in your anger**
> **or discipline me in your wrath.**

Have mercy on me, LORD, for I am faint;
heal me, LORD, for my bones are in agony.
My soul is in deep anguish.
How long, LORD, how long?
Turn, LORD, and deliver me;
save me because of your unfailing love.
Among the dead no one proclaims your name.
Who praises you from the grave?
I am worn out from my groaning.
All night long I flood my bed with weeping
and drench my couch with tears.
My eyes grow weak with sorrow;
they fail because of all my foes.
Away from me, all you who do evil,
for the LORD has heard my weeping.
The LORD has heard my cry for mercy;
the LORD accepts my prayer.
All my enemies will be overwhelmed with shame and anguish;
they will turn back and suddenly be put to shame" (Psalm 6:1-10 NIV Biblegateway).

Later that morning, I went into Doctor G's office. This time, I was solo because Joe had gone off to work. I knew immediately something was wrong.

The look on Doctor G's face when he removed the bandages was, well—shall I say—priceless? Unfortunately, it confirmed my worst fear. The skin and tissue on my right breast were simply too damaged to support the implant and were ripping apart.

I have to hand it to Doctor G. He didn't miss a beat, and immediately had a back-up plan—Latissimus Flap—to keep the implant in. A Latissimus Flap is a procedure in which the surgeon cuts the back muscle, or latissimus, on three sides leaving it attached at a point under the armpit. He then rotates the muscle and flips it over to the chest side in order to create a pocket for the implant. Basically, it adds more tissue and "meat" to the area so that my pathetic skin there could have a chance to heal. Sometimes surgeons use the patient's own body fat to fill the pocket. I could have kissed Doctor G when he told me I didn't have enough. Instead, he would use an implant, either the one I currently had or a smaller one. Now I beg to differ about the body fat—I'm certain I have enough in my butt and abs—but it was a singular, light-hearted moment in an otherwise crappy morning.

We went over the pros and cons of the procedure, but truthfully, I heard only about half the conversation. I was focused on the fact that I had had another surgical failure. I had always trusted Doctor G. I knew he was an expert and one of the leading plastic surgeons in our area. I knew he had done the procedure many times on patients with tissue and skin damage, usually from cancer-related radiation treatments. But I just couldn't figure out why my healthy, non-cancerous side wouldn't heal. How did it manage to stay sewn together the whole summer while I trained for the triathlon? I suppose my answer was that the triathlon was *definitely* a gift from God. Thank you again, Lord!

I was so scared listening to Doctor G. I didn't want to go through another surgery. I begged him to stitch me up to give it one more shot to heal. "I just can't, Kari," he said. "The skin is so pathetic. It won't hold. We need to get you into surgery as soon as possible because there is a big gaping hole in the side of you. If we don't get you closed up sooner rather than later, you will develop some sort of infection like staph or strep."

I reluctantly agreed. On the positive side, the tissue sample taken during surgery two weeks earlier showed no evidence of *mycobacterium Senegalense,* or any other "pond scum" for that matter. But I was concerned about the invasiveness of the procedure. I am an active person. I still like to play. Would cutting off a major muscle limit me?

Doctor G explained that the teres major, another muscle of the back, would compensate for my lost latissimus, so I would eventually be able to ski and swim again and even take up playing golf and tennis if I really wanted to. In other words, the long term prognosis was favorable. I wouldn't be too physically limited after a lot of hard work and rehabilitation, except that I would probably never be able to swing from trees, go rock climbing, or swim the butterfly any longer. Oh, darn! He also reassured me that I would not be deformed. There would be a small scar on my back, but an observer wouldn't notice that I only had one latissimus muscle unless they were really looking for it. Backless dresses and swimming suits were still part of my future—not that I really cared.

Nurse R came in a few minutes later to tell me that the surgery had been scheduled for the next afternoon. Normally, Nurse R is a very strong, stoic person, but I could see her well up with grief. She hugged me and consoled me. She told me that, after all I've been through in the last year, the Latissimus Flap procedure really wouldn't be as hard as it seemed. She discussed how the recovery would be a lot like the original bilateral mastectomy; however, since there aren't as many nerves in the back, it wouldn't hurt quite as bad.

I was beginning to feel like a surgical expert. This would be my sixth in only fourteen months!

At this point, the surgery wasn't even about a boob. It was about fixing a big gaping hole in my side that wouldn't heal. It was about salvaging the last fourteen months. If my left side had been having all these problems also, I would have lopped off both implants. *Flat-chested girl, here I come!* But because I had one side that had healed normally (and no one wanted to touch that), I was stuck. I was stuck on the belief that I could heal. I felt like if I gave in now and had the left side taken off, it would be akin to throwing in the towel. I would lose all the hope I was clinging to. It was time to fix my chest once and for all.

Again, this was not about a boob. If you've had breast cancer, you get it. If you've had reconstructive failures, you surely get it. But for all you supporters out there—no offense and please don't take this the wrong way—please reserve judgment. Love your breast cancer survivor. But please don't say things like, "It's just a boob," "Maybe you should consider prosthetics?" or "Is it worth your vanity over your health?" Believe it or not, I heard all these things. It's tough to describe the emotional turmoil, fright, embarrassment, and self-esteem issues a woman with breast cancer faces. I just couldn't believe that my heavenly father would want me to be permanently lopsided.

I have never believed that God would curse his children, either. But how could this be a blessing? The only thought I could surmise, one that I still cling to tightly, is that God was developing in me a patience and strength I couldn't have fathomed before all this went down. I prayed that if I was being too vain he would show me. I wanted him to be blatantly obvious with me. But more than anything, I wanted his will to be done.

Nonetheless, that whole day I cried. I was so broken. So scared. Despite the doctor's optimism, I had an abysmal track record with my past surgeries. I had little hope. I was terrified that cutting a major muscle would deform me. I was terrified that I would end up permanently lopsided with no arm or back strength on my right side. After all, I hadn't healed like I was supposed to with any of my previous surgeries after chemo. The road ahead seemed like a dead end.

My feelings and emotions were all over the place, more than normal. I started to think the unthinkable: *why did I continue to draw close to God?* It seemed like the closer I got to him, the harder the attacks from Satan came. It would be easier just to abandon my roles of expanding God's kingdom and living out the story of the gospel. Should I live the rest of my life fat, dumb, and happy? Was all this worth it?

Thankfully, I came to my senses. God reminded me once again that I was in a war, and Satan's attacks are ruthless and unceasing. He wants nothing more than to destroy me and you, back us down, and prevent us from living for God.

I really, really, tried to hold thoughts captive and make them obedient to Christ. I cried out, pleaded, and praised him—all in the same breath. ***"When I am afraid, I will trust in you"*** (Psalm 56:3 NIV) and ***"Having hope will give you courage"*** (Job 11:18) were two verses I kept repeating to myself and saying, "I will *still* praise you, Lord, even if the healing doesn't come."

It was difficult to tell our kids when they came home from school that I would, once again, be having surgery—the third surgery in two weeks! I could see the terror in their eyes. It took every ounce of strength I had not to break down and cry. I knew I needed to just love on them. I knew God was growing their strength and patience, too. I knew he had amazing plans to use this godly patience and strength in them one day.

Since the surgery was scheduled for the next day and I knew I would have to spend the night at the hospital, we scrambled to make the necessary preparations. I'm so impressed with the generosity of all our friends. They filled our every need: childcare, meals, prayers. Joe and I had a previously scheduled date that night, and because of the blessing of friends, we were able to get everything ready for the next day and still go out. Every breath is a gift!

Joe and I went out to dinner and to a one-night-only showing of Kirk Cameron's movie *Unstoppable*. Talk about divine timing! This documentary was exactly what we needed. The film addressed the age-old question: if God is a loving god, and if he's in control of everything and can heal anyone at any time, then why does he allow bad things to happen?

Admittedly, it's a tough question to answer. The film kept taking me back to the point that our God loves us so much that he redeemed us from our sin and wretchedness by allowing his only son to suffer and die on a cross. No matter what I was going through, I would never experience that kind of pain. No matter how bad things got for me, it would pale in comparison to the suffering Christ endured. Yet, despite our worst tragedies, he gives us the greatest hope of all—eternal life with him. To sum it all up: for us that know Christ, this world is the closest to hell we will ever get. But for those of us who *don't* know Christ, this world is the closest to heaven we will ever get.

No matter what we are going through, God continues to pursue us. He continues to seek a love relationship with us. He wants us to choose life, not death. But, just like any good parent, he gives us the choice. Our God is greater, our God is stronger, and our God is higher than any other. He is unstoppable! Life is greater than death. Hope is greater than fear. Faith is greater than doubt.[14] I thanked God for reminding me of these truths on a day that had otherwise been filled with fear and doubt. Once again, he gave me what I needed when I needed it. *Thank you, Jesus!* That night, Joe and I went to bed praying and thanking God that things weren't as hopeless as they seemed.

The next morning I awoke with such a great sense of peace and joy. The day before seemed like a bad dream. I knew I still faced surgery that afternoon, but I felt like everything would be okay. I can't explain why I felt that way. I only knew that I was filled with God's peace which, of course, transcends all understanding. I kept thinking of the verse in Psalms which talks about weeping remaining for the night but joy coming in the morning, or in the *mourning*, in my case. For the life of me, I couldn't remember what the specific verse was. I knew Satan was furiously trying to steal my hope that day, and every time I started to get scared I'd repeat out loud, "In the name of Jesus, you have no power over me, Satan! I am resisting you and you *have* to flee!"

After my pre-surgery antibacterial shower, I decided to remove my bandage and take a look at what was underneath. "Holy cow!", "Oh my goodness!", and "Shit!" were a few of the phrases that unwittingly came out of my mouth. I could see a big black area under my breast. At first I thought it was blood pooling, but upon closer observation I realized I was staring right into my body cavity at the implant itself! The skin around it had literally melted away. It looked like someone had tried to cover a large object with an insufficient amount of wet dough. I now knew exactly why Doctor G had looked so panicked the day before and why he couldn't just stitch me up again. There was nothing there to stitch!

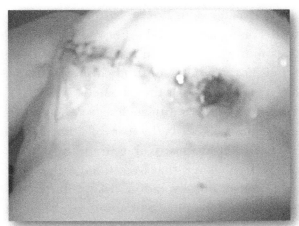

"All the king's horses and all the king's men, couldn't put
Kari together again. But, she knows a KING who can!"
Literally tearing apart at the seams.

Pre-op was the longest ninety minutes ever! I had to re-tell my story a hundred times while fending off the nurses that wanted to stick an IV in my left arm. (Since I had lymph nodes removed on my left side during the mastectomy, I had to make sure that all future IV's, blood draws, and blood pressure readings were done on my *right* side.) Despite the busyness, I was still filled with a sense of peace and joy. No doubt I was scared. ***"But when I am afraid, I will put my trust in you"*** (Psalm 56:3). I had hope, and ***"Having hope will give you courage"*** (Job11:18).

Doctor G came in to mark me and to tell us what he was about to do. I asked if I could hug him. I never blamed him that I couldn't stay glued together. In fact, I appreciated his continued devotion to getting me well. I had been such a source of frustration for him that I wondered if he would write a book, *The Patient That Would <u>Not</u> Heal*. I was confident I was doing the right thing and happy to be in such good hands.

As we were praying with our pastor, Joe noticed a familiar face walk by our cubicle. "Isn't that the nurse who prayed with us last year before your mastectomy?" he asked. At first I wasn't sure; but when someone called him Bruce, we knew it was the same guy. I saw him again as they were wheeling me into the operating room. I explained how my husband had recognized him as a prayer warrior for us last year. Bruce was so impressed we remembered him. He prayed for me, and then asked if he could go out to pray with Joe. He reminded me of the verse in Psalm 91 that God charges his angels to guard over us in all our ways.

In the operating room, I remember trying to answer the questions my nurse and anesthesiologist were asking me but finding it extremely difficult to move my mouth as the tunnel of unconsciousness closed in. I remember both of them saying, "It's okay, Kari. Just rest."

The next thing I knew was I was coming to. And Jesus was right there hanging on to me. There was a bright light. I couldn't see anything or anyone. I could hear familiar voices all around me. I remember telling Nurse R and Doctor G that I loved them and thanking everyone in the room. I remember Doctor G saying that things looked good—all clean, no fluid, no infection. Success. I remember feeling peace and having the verse on my heart: *"May your unfailing love rest upon us, O LORD, even as we put our hope in you"* (Psalm 33:22 NIV). I remember feeling and believing that, this time, the surgery was going to work.

My overnight recovery went well except that my resting heart rate periodically dropped to about thirty three beats per minute. This freaked the night nurse out but the anesthesiologist confirmed that, for me, an "athlete" (ha-ha), it was normal.

Doctor G came by the next morning to examine me. He gave me the thumbs up. "Now go home and heal!" he said.

I felt great, and confident, as I rested at home later that morning. As the day wore on, though, I started to develop a slight fever, hitting 101.5 degrees at one point in the middle of the night. Even though I probably should have called the doctor at that point, I decided there was no need to cause more drama. I took some Tylenol and tried to sleep. I figured the fever was part of the whole post-op thing, so I wasn't too concerned. I decided to wait until the morning to call Doctor G's office. By then, my bandages were soaked through, but I was draining fine from my back and front incisions. I was really uncomfortable and couldn't sleep. Every time I drifted off, I would see a bright light and would become over-whelmed with the sensation that this was the end. But I wasn't scared. I didn't cry. I just continued to feel Jesus' presence, his hope, and his comfort. I continued to trust and to praise God.

I noticed a text from my friend, Tonja, with the same verse I was try-ing to reference the day of the surgery: *"For his anger lasts only a moment, but his favor lasts a lifetime; weeping may remain for a night, but rejoicing comes in the morning"* (Psalm 30:5 NIV). I believed it!

I felt bad for my poor husband. I knew he wanted to stay home with me, but I also knew he needed to get away from all of this. I convinced him to go to work and asked my best friend, Holly, to come sit with me that day. Joe's mom was set to come out and help the following week, so he could get back to work full time. He needed some normalcy in his life, and I was not helping him in my current, fragile state. Again, peace, joy, and comfort flooded over me. Although I physically didn't feel well, I felt okay emotionally and now wanted *him* to get some healing. That is why it is so important to take care of the caregiver. Being a caregiver is a full time job, one that requires a lot of strength. If you know anyone who is a caregiver, pray about some way to give them respite. They need it.

The rest of the day was as normal as we could make it. Holly and her hubbie, Pastor Mike, brought over lunch. Another beautiful church lady friend brought over dinner. The kids and I hung out, and I rested. As I lay down that night, it felt like I was dripping, but the area around the incision remained intact. (I was wearing white to make it quickly notice-able if I *did* leak.) I had no idea why I kept feeling this sensation since there were no visible signs that anything was wrong. My fever was gone. Satan messing with me again, I guess. I begged God for his mercy and protection. *Please, Father. Please, hold me together!*

Normally, I am not *this* dramatic. In fact, I don't like a whole lot of drama in my life. It just seemed like my ordeal wouldn't end. No matter what we did, this hellacious road wouldn't end!

- **Written September 24, 2013, 12:51 P.M.: Okay, NOT Final Surgery**

Dear Family and Friends,

Guess the plans have changed. I thought I was done with all of this, but God's got another chapter to write. Unfortunately, I have not been able to heal from the last surgery, so I will have surgery tomorrow at 1:30 P.M. I am beginning to feel like Humpty Dumpty. All the king's horses and all the king's men can't put me together again! However, I know that our KING can put me together. This earthly tent may keep tearing, but I am hopeful that God can stitch me back up. Thank you for your prayers. God bless you and love you.

"Having hope will give you courage.
You will be protected and will rest in safety" (Job 11:18).

Today is a new day, a day that You have made, Dear Heavenly Father. I will praise You even if I have to start all over again. Thank You for the hope You have given me.

- **Written September 27, 2013, 9:53 A.M.: And We Wait, Trusting Every Minute in Our LORD!**

"I waited patiently for the LORD to help me,
and he turned to me and heard my cry.
He lifted me out of the pit of despair,
out of the mud and the mire.
He set my feet on solid ground
and steadied me as I walked along.

He has given me a new song to sing,
a hymn of praise to our God.
Many will see what he has done and be amazed.
They will put their trust in the LORD.
Oh, the joys of those who trust the LORD,
who have no confidence in the proud
or in those who worship idols.
O LORD my God, you have performed many wonders
for us.
Your plans for us are too numerous to list.
You have no equal.
If I tried to recite all your wonderful deeds,
I would never come to the end of them" (Psalm 40:1-5).

The surgery on Wednesday went well. Thank you to all of you that helped us scramble at the last minute to get kids, meals and, of course, prayer going.

Now we wait! I woke up out of the surgery very hopeful and with Psalm 33:22 on my mind: **"Let your unfailing love surround us, LORD, for our hope is in you alone."**

The recovery has been okay. Came home yesterday and felt really good but, as the day wore on, started to not feel so well. Developed a fever late afternoon/last night and bandages soaked through, so waiting to see what all of this means. Praise the Lord my fever is gone now, but still not feeling the best. Maybe I just need to be put into a month long coma to heal. I am not doing anything. I really am resting. (Thank you to my awesome hubbie Joe for picking up ALL the slack.) So we just wait, trust in the Lord, and know that EVERY breath is a gift. As my cousin says, hug your loved ones, so we are hugging our loved ones and resting in His faithful love and peace.

Love you, dear family and friends. Thank you for your continued prayers.

In Jesus' Precious Love,
Kari

Fourteen

BE STILL, BE PATIENT, AND WAIT ON THE LORD

The next day, I started to feel better. There had been no fever in about twenty hours. I felt really tired, but I couldn't sleep. That night, I finally got up and found something interesting on a Facebook sight called "Walk with Jesus." It was a short clip about Bill Wiese's book *23 Minutes in Hell*. Wow, what a powerful motivator to tell everyone about Jesus. Mr. Weiss claimed that, although he is a Christian, God allowed him to visit hell so he could come back and tell everyone it is a real place and that there is no rescue from the torture once you're on that side of eternity. It made me sob for the people in my life—people I love—that don't believe in God or don't believe that Jesus is the only way to heaven.

The next morning, the resounding theme going through my mind was "be still, be patient, and wait on the Lord." Four verses were on my mind:

"Be still before the LORD and wait patiently for him" (Psalm 37:7 NIV).
"The Lord will fight for you; you need only to be still" (Exodus 14:14 NIV).

"I waited patiently for the LORD; he turned to me and heard my cry" (Psalm 40:1 NIV).
"'Be still, and know that I am God; I will be exalted among the nations, I will be exalted in the earth'" (Psalm 46:10 NIV).

As I prayed these verses, I noticed a devotion by Dave and Jan Dravecky. They wrote, "Yet for so many people in pain, waiting is the one thing they do—a lot…They discover that life is best observed and cherished in the wait. Our waiting gives God time—time to speak to us, to bring us to reflection, surrender and peace."[15]

Their words reminded me to look for peace, joy, and comfort in the midst of my suffering. Even though I literally felt like I was separating at the seams, falling apart, and dying, at the same time I was sure I was living.

The next few weeks seemed to go by in *slower* than slow motion. I was trying to do as little as possible. I would hold my sides when I sneezed or coughed out of fear of falling apart.

To my great surprise, at both the one and two week post-op appointments, Doctor G proudly announced that I was healing normally. *Healing normally!* No joking way! I hadn't heard those words in over a year! "Okay," I thought. "Breathe, in and out, and thank Jesus." So I did, right then and there, in the surgeon's office. *Thank you, God!*

Soon it was October: Breast Cancer Awareness Month. Last year, I hated October. I was plenty aware of breast cancer! This year, I was excited. I could wear all my pink supporting things again. More importantly, I realized God had given me a voice and a certain credibility as a breast cancer survivor. I got the chance to tell my raw, but real, story—not to hurt or offend anyone, but to let people know it's not all about a cute pink ribbon. Since one out of seven women will contract breast cancer in their lifetimes, I wanted to be real about it. Some people may have thought I was a bitch, although I hope it was only a few. I wanted to make people aware of their words, particularly the friends and loved ones of people battling breast cancer. I wanted to let them know that telling cancer patients it's *only* hair and *only* boobs doesn't comfort them. I wanted them to know how offensive it is to tell someone with cancer that they could have prevented it or that their cancer was probably caused by their own bad habits or the sin in their life. People said all this crap to me. (I really wanted to slap them, too!) Anyway, I wasn't trying to offend any good-intentioned soul, but just trying to make them aware of how powerful their words could be. Believe me, I have definitely put my foot in my mouth many times and still continue to do so. But I also pray that the Holy Spirit reveals this to me when I do so I can apologize.

I know that my boldness came from the voice of experience. Perhaps my "bitchiness" was because I hadn't had a real shower in four weeks! I will never, ever take a shower for granted again! I was *so* happy to finally be able to get back in the shower and ditch the sponge bath.

I wrote this book to encourage the breast cancer survivor. But even more than that, I want to give them a voice—a voice that I didn't always feel I had when I needed it. You know what they say about hindsight. When my dad was dying from stage four lung cancer, he would hold his tongue when people told him stupid shit (pardon my French!). I know because I was one of those people! I said some pretty judgmental crap to him. But now, God had let me see the other side. At first, I too would let people say those silly things, and I would internalize it and get bitter about it. But, through my own cancer experience, God gave me a boldness to speak up and to remind people that sometimes the best thing to say is nothing.

Fifteen

BEAUTY FROM ASHES

At the time of writing this chapter, I'm four weeks post-op and all is well—with my soul, too. I continue to wait on God's perfect timing. His story in me will continue until the day I die. He has allowed me to share a very small, private struggle to encourage other people. I am still too close to all of this to know what my role in his story is, and I may never really know why he chose me to go through all of this. But I *can* say I am completely humbled. I am completely honored. I have seen him use all of this mess to help tell his message. Sitting in the middle of pain and turmoil is never any fun. But what I have to keep reminding myself is that some of the richest verses, stories, and passages in the Bible were told by men and women who were in the middle of a storm. God faithfully stayed with them, helped them, grew them, inspired them, and used them to tell his story and comfort others. I hope that is what he has done with this book. I hope my story has honored God and made you think more about him. I hope this has helped strengthen your belief and relationship with him. I know it has for me. Wow, I can't even imagine having to do this without him.

- **Written October 2, 2013, 5:56 P.M.: Whew!**

One week down! Bandages came off this morning, and I am healing "normally." *Praise You, Jesus!* Keep praying and crossing your fingers that I don't sneeze too hard.

**"God blesses you who weep now,
for in due time you will laugh"** (Luke 6:21).

Afterword: Shine My Light— Out of the Wilderness

$\mathcal{C}$hristmas 2013. Three months after my surgical debacle, all was well and both Joe and I thought it may be time to push forward with the book. It seemed like life was returning to normal. I didn't want to be referred to as the one who had cancer. I knew God allowed this to happen for some reason, but I wanted to separate myself from the last year and a half.

I was taking a drug called Tamoxifin, which suppresses estrogen and helps keep breast cancer from coming back. However, one of its side effects (affecting about 1 in 300 cases) is endometrial cancer. For that reason, patients on Tamoxifin have to have a pelvic ultrasound every year to monitor for endometrial cancer.

I had my pelvic ultrasound scheduled for New Year's Eve. After the test, I knew something was up. The radiology tech would barely look me in the eye. She kept saying I probably wouldn't get the results for a couple days because of the holiday.

As I was walking out I begged God, "If this is something bad, can you *please* let us find out in 2013? I don't want 2014 to be another bad year!"

The rest of the week went on, and I didn't really think of the test until the next week. I remember hearing a song by Chris Tomlin called "Sovereign," and I decided to make it my "heart cry" prayer. "No matter what comes my way Lord, I will trust you." I called the cancer center to see if the results had come back. My doctor had just returned from vacation which is why they hadn't yet called. It seemed that there was a mass on my ovary. *Crap! Seriously?* The doctor wanted me to have an MRI so she could have a better look at it.

I wanted to run. I wanted to pretend that none of this was happening. I wanted to simply forget about it. Of course, that was impossible. So I pulled up my big girl panties and scheduled the MRI. I got in right away for the MRI but had to wait *another* weekend for the results. The wait was excruciating.

I had to distract myself to get through the weekend. We had previously planned some fun special dates with our kids, so I kept praying for God to keep me focused on him and to remain in the moment that he was graciously giving me. I wanted to hold every negative thought captive and to make it obedient to Christ. I prayed for peace, and shared my predicament with all the prayer warriors in my life. Every time I started to freak out, I'd ask God to help me. He did. Sometimes he used his word. Sometimes he used an unsuspecting hug from a friend or family member. But he *did* help me!

The doctor called me personally on Monday afternoon. The MRI indicated an endometrioma, or benign lesion on the ovary. It is sometimes referred to as a "chocolate cyst." But there was nothing I needed to do or any further treatment. *PRAISE THE LORD! PRAISE THE LORD!*

I don't know if this scare happened to remind me not to forget the wilderness I had just come from, or maybe it was to keep me away from doctors' offices permanently. (Just kidding—kind of.) But I *do* know that it reminded me to always trust God. In those two weeks of waiting, God brought our family closer-than-close together—again! He rose up hundreds of prayer warriors to pray for a miracle. He had my pastor anoint me with oil and pray for a miracle. Through the wait, God was constantly there showing me his love. Even if I am sick, I can rely on him. He is ever faithful. He loves me like crazy, and he wants the best for his children.

Now, it has been almost two years since I was diagnosed with breast cancer and only a few weeks since my last medical scare. Once again, I had suspicious endometrial cells that turned out to be benign. When I shared the news with my pastor and his family, he said, "It was your faith that healed you!" Wow, that is about the best compliment a girl could ever get. Watch out, mountains! You are moving next!

All totaled, I have twelve scars, three lasting conditions, and two very different crooked breasts—even after six surgeries. But you know what? I don't mind. The scars remind me of God's power, the lasting conditions remind me to stop listening to the world, and the two very different breasts—well, let's just say my husband says he likes variety. And you know what else? I swam the butterfly! Granted, I had fins on, but I swam three very respectable twenty five yard butterflies to celebrate two years of being cancer free. With God, *all* things are possible (Matthew 19:26).

So how does your story fit into God's story? Where are your scars?

As I wrap up *my* story, let me tell you the greatest love story ever told! God pursued us before we were ever born, creating us fearfully and wonderfully made. He knew the plans and purposes of our lives. He knew we would sin. He knew we would need a savior. He loves us so much that he sacrificed his one and only son—a son who had never sinned, the perfect son of God, who *was* God. He gave his son Jesus to the world to teach us. Jesus used his very short time on this earth to teach us about loving his father and loving others. He summed up the Ten Commandments in two simple statements: Love the Lord your God with all your heart, all your soul, all your mind, and all your strength, and love your neighbor as yourself (compiled from Matthew 22:37-39, Mark 12:30-31, and Luke 10:27). Then, *"Because of the joy awaiting him, he endured the cross, disregarding its shame"* (Hebrews 12:2). God turned his crucifixion into a resurrection so we could have eternal life with our Heavenly Father.

Praise to the God of All Comfort

"Praise be to the God and Father of our Lord Jesus Christ, the Father of compassion and the God of all comfort, who comforts us in all our troubles, so that we can comfort those in any trouble with the comfort we ourselves receive from God. For just as we share abundantly in the sufferings of Christ, so also our comfort abounds through Christ. If we are distressed, it is for your comfort and salvation; if we are comforted, it is for your comfort, which produces in you patient endurance of the same sufferings we suffer. And our hope for you is firm, because we know that just as you share in our sufferings, so also you share in our comfort" (2 Corinthians 1:3-7 NIV Biblegateway).

"Obviously, I'm not trying to win the approval of people, but of God. If pleasing people were my goal, I would not be Christ's servant" (Galatians 1:10).

O LORD, if you heal me, I will be truly healed;
if you save me, I will be truly saved.
My praises are for you alone!

Jeremiah 17:14

... and I truly believe.

A Letter to You, the
Cancer Survivor

I've been thinking a lot about you and praying for you. Right now, it's hard. Everyone around you wants to help, tries to comfort you, and tries to encourage you by saying something positive. But I bet sometimes you want to tell them to go to hell! Cancer sucks!

There is no sugar coating it. You know it and feel it in every inch of your body. I think sometimes people want to sugar coat sadness and then get upset when the person that is actually fighting cancer won't buy into their optimism. They call us pessimists when, actually, we are realists. We're simply allowing the honesty and rawness of life to help us feel and experience our emotions.

So I'm giving you permission—not that you need it—to be raw and honest with what you're feeling and experiencing. Some people around you will get it and will still be there for you. Some won't and will be hurt that you didn't take their "encouragement." They'll try to make your cancer about them and not about you. And some will have a story about their own experience with a spouse, sibling, or long-lost cousin to which I say—hum to yourself! I mean it, hum! Usually, the person means well and is trying to help, but if their story doesn't really pertain to your situation (and usually they don't) just hum a song in your head and smile. This was some of the best advice one of my mentors gave me.

Above all, just be! Let all—yes all—your feelings happen. Capture them in a journal, paint it on canvas or ceramic, or express them in some way. Allow them to happen.

I do believe there is a gift in sorrow and a present in sadness. It's deep, it's real, it's wild, and it allows you to see life differently, and that's totally okay!

I don't know how you feel about God or Jesus, but I do know that God loves you! Some really crappy things happen in life because this world belongs to the evil one, the devil. But regardless of what happens, God does love you and has a plan for you, ***"plans for good and not for disaster, to give you a future and a hope"*** (Jeremiah 29:11).

So if you ever want to talk more about God and Jesus and their love for us, I'd love to talk! But if you don't, that's okay, too. It's part of who I am, so I apologize if I talk about God all the time. I'm just so very grateful for all the blessings He's given me. But I do know God expects this world to suck sometimes, yet He still sends us love notes: an amazing full moon, a glorious sunrise, a sweet gesture from your spouse, or a cheery smile and hug from your kids.

By the way, if you ever want to see emotions run amuck, check out some of David's writings in Psalms. His feelings are all over the place but—boy, oh boy—can I relate!

Love you. God bless you. Thank you for allowing me to be transparent and vulnerable.

Kick this cancer in the ass!

In Jesus' Precious Love,
Kari

To contact me or if you have questions or just want to say hello, please drop me an email at: mytriplemastectomy@yahoo.com or visit me on my Facebook page: https://www.facebook.com/Mytriplemastectomy

Acknowledgments

I know I am going to forget to thank someone, and for that I am truly sorry. But if you know me, I can safely say you helped me. So, thank you!

I would like to thank, first and foremost, our Heavenly Father and His Son Jesus, the Savior of the World. I can't wait to see eternity on Your Holy side but, until then, thank You for all the blessings on this side of eternity.

To J, my editor. Thank you for saying "yes" to this project, as if you didn't already have enough to do! It had to be you to edit this. You have walked this journey with me closer than anyone else. Thank you for never once letting go of my hand.

To my kiddos, sorry you and Daddy had to go through all of this. I know God is using this for our good. Sorry and thank you for all the times I had to ignore you and let you be "big kids" during the writing and editing of this book. Thank you for letting us tell our story.

Karen, thank you for your professional editing advice. Thank you also for your mentorship and sisterhood, and thank you for driving out of state and out of your way *just* to pray with me in person the night before my double mastectomy.

Carolyn, thank you for the extra set of eyes and being my "grammar technician." I am hoping this project was more of a distraction than a burden. You and David are ROCK STARS in your faith. Thank you for letting God shine through you both in some of your darkest hours.

D.J., thank you for your professional author advice and encouragement. You are an amazing person!

Holly and Mike: Holly you were there from before day one and challenged me to think "Why *not* me?" You've encouraged me to "go, fight, win!" even when I had no more fight in me, and then you reminded me where my strength really comes from. I love you so much, soul sis and "breast" friend! Mike, thank you for all the deep conversations about death, fear, and life. Thank you for my "Captive" sweatshirt that I lived in on this journey. Your friendship and brotherhood means the world to me.

Rachel, thank you for all the miles we logged and for your ear and oncology knowledge. Thank you for always being there for me, even during one of the hardest times in your life. Thank you also for encouraging me not to let this book sit too long, as the raw emotions get watered down and the realness of the raw emotions would be lost.

Kathy, thank you for all the wonderful and wise advice. Your friendship, sistership, and mentorship have been completely priceless.

Kathy, thank you for the countless hours you helped me by watching Jewels, and for the meals you sent home with her. You are such a blessing!

Liesl, thank you for dropping everything in Washington D.C. at the Pentagon just to come check on me yourself.

Pastor Mike, Pastor Rob, Pastor Dave, Chaplain Tonja and the whole River family and Worship Team: thank you. You have helped keep our family afloat when we felt like we were sinking. Tony, Annette, and the youth group, thank you for making us one of your service projects. River, *you* are the Acts 2 church to us. Thank you for all the songs and verses you've passed along to encourage us. You are our family and we love you.

200th Airlift Squadron, thank you for all the gift cards, meals, and, of course, love and prayers. You are our family, too, and we love you.

Lesley and Jennifer, thank you for making sure my family had food during chemo weeks when food was the *last* thing on my mind.

Craig and Meredith, your unfailing love and mercy through *Jesus Callings*, dinners, and vino always came at the perfect time. Thank you for loving us so lavishly! Thank you.

Trina and Les, thank you and your boys for the chemo basket, gift cards, lotions, and all your medical advice. Thanks for checking on me after-hours and for your fundraising wine dinner for us. Your generosity and compassion are overwhelming.

Lisa, thank you for your chemo care package, too. I am sorry you were all too familiar with the good things to have during chemo, but you nailed it! I used EVERYTHING you gave me, and was very thankful for it. Thanks also for naming my guitar and introducing me to the "Singing Nun."

Jensen's and Broken Bones BBQ, thank you for all the meals you brought over. We are definitely carnivores.

Kim, thank you for all your prayers, texts, and emails. Thanks also for assuring me that the new "girls" are going to be okay. Thank you also for giving me an opportunity to meet Suzan to encourage her on her walk.

Stephanie, thank you for your weekly encouraging cards and e-mails. Your support never wavered.

Gail, thank you for my "super hero" cape. It helped me in more ways than you will know.

Julie, thank you for all your advice and for all your wigs and hats and scarfs. You saved us hundreds of dollars by letting me borrow that stuff while my cranium was bald.

Traci, thank you for ALWAYS having a smile on your face, and always bringing me enCOURAGEment. Dave, thanks for allowing God to always present the perfect message through your desire to serve Him.

Clay and Shawna, thank you for the prayers, and chapter title and cover ideas. Thank you also for believing in me and honoring me by asking me to speak at the grassRoots Ladies' Day Conference, my first keynote speaking event.

Malia, Derek, and family, you ROCK! Who does a triathlon just to cheer someone on?! You are all amazing and I loved being an IRONGIRL with you, Malia. Let's do it again. Derek, your bike is kick-ass!

Own Your Own Health (OYOH), your mission of helping people "own their own health" has made ALL the difference through this treatment. Thank you for what your nonprofit stands for and for giving a voice to the patient.

To my family and my Ward Zoo family, thank you. Thanks for all the reminders to "fight like a girl" and for being my biggest fan club. Thank you to my moms who dropped everything to help our family out. Thanks to all my brothers and sisters and nephews and nieces and cousins who made life bearable in the pits and who reminded me that we all have our struggles. John and Lisa, you are miracles, and I am forever grateful for what God has done and is doing in your lives.

Thank you to all my wonder sisters in Christ from Japan and Yokota Air Base. You helped shape my early years as a Christian, wife, mom, and friend. Thank you to those of you who encouraged me to journal and to those of you who mentored me.

Thank you to all of my mentors—the ones who helped me grow as a wife, mom, sister in Christ, and friend. Thank you for encouraging me to keep writing and for challenging me to live outside my comfort zone.

To all my survivor friends, thank you for your voice, your opinions, and your rawness. Your story helped shape mine. Thank you.

Appendix 1

HEAD SHAVING PARTY

One of my mentors, sisters-in-Christ, friend, and two-time breast cancer survivor told me about what she did when her hair was falling out. She told me her hair never came out in big clumps, but reached a point where it simply died. She decided to have her two girls help with the process of getting rid of her dead hair. So, they had a celebratory hair cutting party. Both of her girls grabbed their scissors and helped their mom get rid of that dead chemo hair.

I loved this so much, we decided to do the same. And, like my friend, my hair never came out in clumps; instead, it started to die and literally break off about two weeks after my first chemo. I lamented all day about shaving it. I wasn't ready, but I knew my hair was already dead and quickly breaking off at the ends. So that day after school, my three girls got their scissors and cut away. When they got it short enough, my son grabbed the shears and shaved my head. He had so much fun doing that. Finally, my dear husband got the straight razor and shaving cream and shaved my head all the way down to the scalp.

It was a bittersweet night. We celebrated with a cake after the shaving. I was so glad my family helped me with one of the first big hurdles of chemo.

"Let's do this!"
Getting ready
for the shave

My cape of courage.

The girls starting the
first wave of cutting

"Shorter please!"

"Here comes the
sheers. Yikes!"

My men shaving me

Team Ward and G.I.K!

Appendix 2

Iron Girl—ALL Things are Possible with God

I supernaturally stayed "glued" together. God blessed me with this really fun day!

Malia and I warming up. The water was much colder than the air.	"Go!"	Transition #1

The finish! "Thank You, Lord!"

Team Ward

"Iron Girls"
Thanks Malia!

Appendix 3

BOOB RECONSTRUCTION

These pictures aren't meant to be salacious, but I want to be real with my fellow breast cancer survivors facing reconstruction. I know I was very curious as to what was going to happen, and very scared when things didn't go as planned.

Initial reconstruction consult: someone's excited!

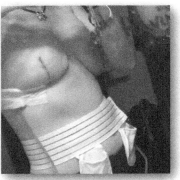

Double Mastectomy

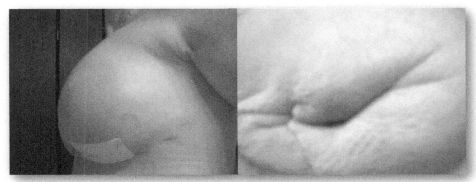

"A Walk in the Park":
Two implants go in…

…one comes out:
"Deflated-Nipple Soufflé"

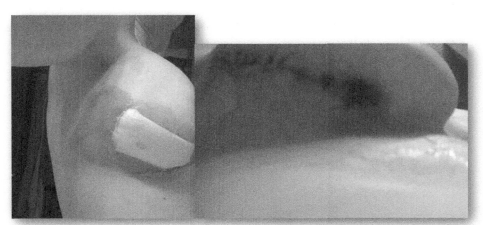

Let's try this again…
second implant in.

Big gaping hole. The black area is
actually the bottom of the implant.

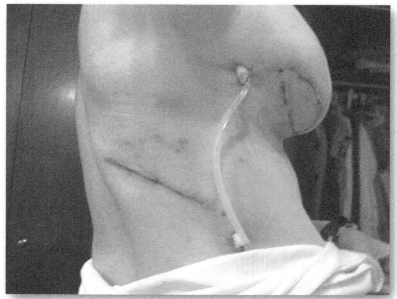

Post-Latissimus Flap procedure.

Appendix 4

The "Backstory" CaringBridge Entries

(These are my uncensored and unedited words from the caringbridge. org website page I created after my cancer diagnosis. Please forgive any grammatical or punctuation-related errors. The rawness of these CaringBridge entries conveys my state of mind when they were written, and is reflective of the roller coaster of moods and emotions I experienced throughout my cancer journey.)

- **Written June 7, 2012 for my CaringBridge Title Page**

Never thought I would be authoring a CaringBridge site for myself, but with all the love that has been poured into us and all that want to pray and help, I just thought this might be the best way to keep you "abreast" of the situation. Laugh, it's funny and it's okay!

Breast Cancer. That was the diagnosis we received 6 June at about 3 pm. The adventure is just beginning, and before it get's too busy, I wanted to just journal how it began.

A few weeks ago, I noticed a dimple in my left breast. I had a Dr.'s appointment scheduled the end of May and was going to just bring it up then. I felt no lump. The only reason I thought I should bring it up with my Dr. was because at my annual mammo in Jan (which was normal), the mammo tech uttered words that I know now were divine conversation, about the visual inspection of your breasts, and if there is any sort of asymmetry have them checked. The dimple was only on one side of one breast, not on the other breast, so the asymmetry over-ruled my thoughts of "oh it's just gravity and old age." I have never heard or read these words before in all my years of self-breast exams, so I am blessed that this woman gave me that knowledge, otherwise I may have thought anything of it until my next mammo. Ladies keep an eye on your "girls" and any dimples have checked out.

The Dr.'s appointment referred to an ultrasound. Still not thinking this was anything, after all I have fibrous breasts. The ultrasound was referred to a diagnostic mammogram, and the Dr. came in to tell me there was a "suspicious" mass they wanted to biopsy. I knew my life was getting ready to change when I checked in for the biopsy and on the clipboard with my file I saw a postee note that read: "Fast Track" and the results were here before we could even take a deep breath.

Monday 11 June, we will meet with oncology and the surgeon, we are so hopeful and blessed that both are "breast cancer specialists." I've even been assigned a "breast navigator" to help be a patient advocate who will be with us from start to finish, an extra set of eyes and ears for us, and a source to go to.

So until then we really don't know much. EXCEPT that we have been completely overwhelmed, humbled and in awe at God's love reaching down to us through His Word the Bible, family and friends prayers and encouraging words, and all the little "love notes" God has placed all around us.

Seems so ironic that last year at this time, my family, my bestie Holly and I were getting ready to do the Avon walk for breast cancer, I guess all I can say is we are STILL IN IT TO END IT! And God's ways are not our ways...and I am thankful for that.

Oh Father God, THANK YOU! I am completely humbled and overwhelmed by the amount of LOVE and PEACE You have poured into our lives this week. Thank You for extending Your open arms, through Your True Word, family and friends, and all the "love notes" you have placed in our lives these last few days. Your loving arms are a safe refuge, THANK YOU! I Love You! Thank You!

"Let all that I am wait quietly before God,
for my hope is in him.
He alone is my rock and my salvation,
my fortress where I will not be shaken.
My victory and honor come from God alone.
He is my refuge, a rock where no enemy can reach me.
O my people, trust in him at all times.
Pour out your heart to him,
for God is our refuge" (Psalm 62:5-8).

Feeling small the day after we got the diagnosis, and trying to enjoy the "normal" of everyday life before the storm comes.

- **Written June 8, 2012, 6:11 A.M.**

Dear Cancer,

We have never met personally before now. Yes, you have rudely invaded too many of my family and friends' bodies and, yes, that was personal. But until now, I have been avoiding a personal relationship with you.

Okay, so now that we are introduced, let me take this opportunity to tell you a few things about me.

Don't ever think that I'm going to let you take over my life. I have the power of Christ in me. In fact, **"[His] power is made perfect in [my] weakness"** (2 Corinthians 12:9 NIV).

I'd be lying if I said I wasn't scared, but **"when I am afraid, I will trust in [God]"** (Psalm 56:3 NIV) and **"I will not be afraid for [God is] close beside me"** (Psalm 23:4).

I learned a promise from God when you visited my dad two years ago. He told me, **"Never will I leave you; never will I forsake you"** (Hebrews 13:5 NIV).

So again, I have the power of Christ made perfect in any weakness you insert into my body. Oh, and did I tell you I am a fighter? I have the *full armor of God* accessible whenever I remember to dress in it (Ephesians 6:10-18).

Also:

I am a witness: **"Let the redeemed of the LORD say so"** (Psalm 107:2 KJV). So!

I am a warrior: **"May the praise of God be in their mouths and a double-edged sword in their hands"** (Psalm 149:6 NIV).

I am a bride of Christ: Isaiah 61:10, Isaiah 62:4, and Zephaniah 3:17.

And the best promise of all: **"The LORD will fight for [me]; [I] need only to be still"** (Exodus 14:14 NIV).

And even if you win this battle in my body, my "earthly tent," you can't even come close to touching me in the eternal body God made for me (2 Corinthians 5:1).

So there! My dukes are up. I'm ready to fight! Again, even if you win this earthly fight, Christ has already won the eternal battle. I am His, and He promised a kingdom that is unshakable. For that I am thankful, and I worship my Father God with holy fear and awe (Hebrews 12:28).

Dear Holy Father,

Thank you that I am yours and thank you that you've got me in the palm of your hand. I love you!

"May the words of my mouth and the meditation of my heart be pleasing to you, O LORD, my rock and my redeemer" *(Psalm 19:14). Thank You for the grace, mercy, and forgiveness You give me and Thank You that You gave it ALL, fought the worst fight so a sinner like me could be with you. Thank You. I Love You My Lord.*

K

A pic my daughter took when my friend Lesley found out about my diagnosis.

• Written June 11, 2012, 11:35 P.M.: First Appointment

Hello Everyone! It's Joe here, writing for Kari. Today we met both the oncologist and breast surgeon for the first time. It felt like a crash course on cancer wrapped in acronyms and treatment options. I was reminded just how much my brain has shrunk since having kids...or becoming a pilot. Fortunately, our "breast navigator" Cindy (that's really her job title) sat in on the appointment as an active observer and note taker. (I kind of wish I had such a person when I was a student at the Academy, although I'm sure the Air Force would have forced me to call her something different.) Anyway, we're very thankful that Cindy will serve as our cancer expert and personal liaison to all the different specialties involved in Kari's treatment. In a nut-shell, both doctors were very optimistic about Kari's prognosis. Although the cancer has invaded a large section of her left breast, it doesn't appear that it has spread to the rest of her body. Unfortunately, she'll probably need a full mastectomy followed by four months of chemotherapy. We're still waiting for the results of a few remaining tests before the doctors can nail down a specific treatment time line. In the meantime, we'll patiently wait (Psalm 37:7) and bask in the comfort of knowing so many people are praying for us. Thank you for that. Kari's spirits have been high, and I'm proud of her for handling a sucky situation with abundant class and grace. She wanted me to keep this update light by ending with a boob joke, but I just couldn't think of anything that wasn't too titillating. So, for now I'll simply say good night and thank you for supporting us.

- **Written June 15, 2012, 7:23 A.M.**

Today I'm a 10 day breast cancer SURVIVOR! Praise the Lord! I had no idea that the dating of surviving starts the day of diagnosis, but it makes sense...I'm not dead yet...I'm Surviving. And Praise the Lord that we have a GREAT SAVIOR that helps us survive.

No new news, just waiting on tests to come back, and patiently waiting on the LORD to direct our steps in this. Thank you for your prayers and thoughts, we are feeling them and we have been so encouraged and inspired.

Today, Joe has a Denver overnight, so the kids and I are going to "escape" up to the hotel and hang out with him tonight. Joe and I decided this will be a "cancer-free" excursion, we all need a break from all this cancer talk, I think especially the kids. They are doing well, but they need a break from it. My heart breaks for all those who can't take a "break" from it. Thank You LORD that You have allowed us this reprieve.

"Praise the LORD, O my soul;
all my inmost being, praise his holy name" (Psalm 103:1 NIV).

In the KJV it reads:

"Bless the LORD, O my soul:
and <u>all</u> that is within me, bless his holy name" (Psalm 103:1 KJV, emphasis added).

A verse that has been "tattooed" (with sharpie) on my hand this last week: **"May the praise of God be in their mouths and a double-edged sword in their hands"** (Psalm 149:6 NIV).

This verse has been my desire and focus this last week as life gets "shaken up" a little for our household. Despite what happens, I need to PRAISE our Holy Father!

Like the theme from the movie *Facing the Giants*, we need to praise Him when we win and we need to praise Him when we lose so that ALL the Glory goes to God. (I'm terrible with movie quotes, so you'll have to watch the movie to get the exact wording...great movie).

It's a GREAT day to PRAISE the LORD!

I borrowed this from a sweet teen in our church who LOVES THE LORD, too, and she said I could use it:

"Just a nobody
wanting Everybody
to know about a SOMEBODY!"

- **Written June 17, 2012, 1:34 P.M.**

    "But as for me and my household, we will serve the LORD" (Joshua 24:15 NIV).

    I am so thankful that I have a husband that is following God's lead in our lives and is leading his family to follow and serve the Lord too. Thank you, J. I Love You! God Bless you and Happy Father's Day!

    Happy Father's Day to all you Dads, hope you are enjoying this day that the Lord made, rejoicing and celebrating every breath! We just want to thank you all for all the prayers and thoughts, sweet notes on CaringBridge and Facebook, cookies, phone calls, support...oh that reminds me, I have a boob joke:

    Q: What do toys and ***boobs*** have in common?
    A: They were both originally made for kids, but dad ends up playing with them! Happy Father's Day!

    Thank you for everything, and please know as you are praying for us, interceding for our family, we are also praying for you and your family. Praying that you know HOW much your Holy Heavenly Father Loves and adores you.

Happy Father's Day God! Thank you for these family and friends you have blessed us with. Please Bless them Father, bless them Indeed! Amen.

God Bless you.

In Jesus' Precious Love,
Kari

- **Written June 22, 2012, 8:47 A.M.**

Reading *Crazy Love* by Francis Chan and came across this today, words from my own heart scripted by another:

> God has allowed hard things in your life so you can show the world that your God is great and that knowing Him brings peace and joy, even when life if hard. Like the psalmist who wrote, "I saw the prosperity of the wicked...Surely in vain have I kept my heart pure... When I tried to understand all this, it was oppressive to me *till I entered the sanctuary of God.*" (Ps. 73:3, 13, 16-17).[16]

Wow! WE have felt so loved and encouraged by so many. Thank You God for these blessings in our life. Thank you Dear family and friends. Thank you for your continued prayers. I want to ask for a HUGE prayer request: For my surgeons, oncologist, nurses, everyone we will meet and will help me get better. Please pray for them, for their relationship with Christ, and for them to know the Love of God. Pray for them to be blessed.

Speaking of the medical team that is helping us, my surgery is scheduled for Monday 9 July, bilateral mastectomy. We will meet with the oncologist and genetic counselor to go over the MRI and genetic test results, however it won't really matter as far as the surgery is concerned since I am opting for a double mastectomy, but it will matter in the treatment route and for future things. I did find out I am ER/PR positive and Her2 positive, that determines the treatment route after the chemo. Needless to say, it is a long road ahead of us, but I am so encouraged by God working through people in our lives. Reminds me of one of my favorite songs at the moment, "Carry Me to the Cross" by Kutless.

Yesterday, I had the opportunity to visit with a "Warrior in Christ", Julie, who walked this road last year, I feel like her shadow. I've only known her for a week, but I feel like she is a long lost sister. She is praying with me, informing me, and not sugar coating anything...and she is doing it all with the love of Christ, and showing me all the ways God is using this for HIS Glory. Truthfully after our convo yesterday, I WAS SCARED! YIKES! But it was God that truly orchestrated this because minutes after I left her, she called. I missed the call and returned it later. She told me of a chemo drug that I will probably have to have nicknamed "the red devil." She told me when I heard this, to not think of it as the red devil, but the <u>blood of Christ</u>, pouring into me, cleansing me and defeating this cancer. YAY GOD! I LOVE LOVE LOVE how He works and How the Holy Spirit stirs our hearts to reflect on "breathing life"...Every Breath is a gift as my Sis-in-love Lori would say. I will boldly say "every breast is also a gift!":).

If you are in a hard place in your life, I pray that you will find peace and joy in Our GREAT God. I pray that you will enter His Holy Sanctuary as the Psalmist encourages us to do, and I pray that God's love and peace will just completely engulf you. God Bless you!

Okay now time for the joke of the post:
Q: What did saggy boob say to the other saggy boob?
A: "If we don't get some support here people are going to think were nuts." (My son loved this one.)

Love you and God Bless you,

In Jesus' Precious Love,
Kari

- **Written June 26, 2012, 9:46 P.M.**

Hello Family and Friends, if you have seen the news lately, you know that there are some pretty horrific fires in Colorado, one that started Saturday in South Colorado Springs has definitely turned pretty fierce.

PLEASE PRAY for all those men and women who are risking their lives (in this high 90/100's heat) to put these fires out. Please pray for all those that have been displaced and evacuated and have now today lost homes. Please pray for rain, rain that we most definitely need.

We are fine, we live north of these fires and across the interstate, but it is so sad and surreal to see these huge plumes of smoke and the flames burning the sides of the mountains.

I want to share with you something my cousin-in-law wrote on her husband John's CaringBridge (John is a living miracle and Lisa is an angel of God spreading His love and hope in the middle of their storms). Today in my JESUS CALLING book it said:

Nothing takes Me by surprise. I will not allow circumstances to overwhelm you, so long as you look to Me. I will help you cope with whatever the moment presents.[17]

Holy Father God, I just want to say Thank You for Who You are and What you do. I want to ask for You to come into this situation here in Colorado, the whole state, Dear Father God. We need You! We need Your holy rain to pour down on us. Thank You for helping so many people escape this and for the evacuations, Please give these people comfort and support in this time. Please show us how we can help. Thank You, Father, that You are the God, bigger than all of this and in control of everything, and please help all of us have the peace of knowing that You are always with us. I Love You Father God. In Your Holy Name, Amen.

- **Written June 27, 2012, 9:50 A.M.**

Wow Dear Prayer Warriors,

I'm calling you all Prayer Warriors, because our state needs some bold prayers!

I know I don't need to ask anyone what to pray for, but just ask that we continue to approach the throne of our

Graceful Heavenly Father, boldly, confidently and humbly, with Holy Fear and Awe. These fires are humbling and realistic to how frail all of this life is. But another reminder of How BIG our God is. Our God IS Greater! PRAY BOLDLY!

Thank you for praying, praying without ceasing is what one news caster last night reminded us all to do...PRAISE GOD! Praise God that no human has been harmed.

Holly texted me this this morn and I want to share:

"Though the fig tree does not blossom and there is no fruit on the vines, [though] the product of the olive fails and the fields yield no food, though the flock is cut off from the fold and there are no cattle in the stalls, Yet I will rejoice in the Lord; I will exult in the [victorious] God of my salvation! [Rom 8:37.] The Lord God is my Strength, my personal bravery, and my invincible army; He makes my feet like hinds' feet and will make me to walk [not to stand still in terror, but to walk] and make [spiritual] progress upon my high places [of trouble, suffering, or responsibility]!" (Habakkuk 3:17-19 AMP)

AMEN!

A song that I used to sing as a kid, that came to mind this morning: "Though the mountains may fall and the hills turn to dust, YET the LOVE of the Lord will stand. As a shelter for all, who will call on His name, sing the Praise and the Glory of God!"

This song was written based off of the whole chapter of Isaiah 40 (some amazing promises of encouragement in there).

No matter how bad all of this gets, OUR GOD IS GOOD ALL THE TIME!

- **Written June 28, 2012, 7:06 A.M.**

Well, the last few days have been surreal. But Praise God that He is on His throne and that He loves us.

We are still safe from the fires, they are south and on the west side of I-25. We haven't even been in a pre-evac notice yet, although the west side of Monument has. The Academy is still pressing forward with their in-processing of the class of 2016, so we figure we are safe for the time being.

THANK YOU and Please continue to pray for those fire fighters, forest service, police officers. God Bless them. It has been sad hearing about those who have lost their houses, there is no official count, but the number being thrown around in in the 200's:(.

Praise God that no one has been injured, even when they did a mass evacuation of the Rockrimmon area the other day, crazy pandemonium thousands fleeing down the side of a mountain, and not one injury...THANK YOU GOD!

So updates on this cancer thing. Met with the oncologist, plastic surgeon and genetic counselor this week. Had an echo cardio and a PET scan. I think I have had all the big tests, I've been CT'ed, MRI'ed and now PET'ed. My bilateral (double) mastectomy will be on 9 July. I won't be able to start chemo until I recover (6 weeks later), however I was given the green light to participate in a family reunion the end of July....so come on out Ward Zoo, we've been expecting you. I LOVE how God's timing is perfect, how He is totally blessing us with this trip between losing my "girls" and starting the chemo walk. PRAISE HIM! I was told though that the triathlon I was planning to do on the 22nd of July, was out and I'd have to do it next year. So ladies, I am rallying to get a bunch of people to do the "Tri for the Cure" next summer.

My Jesus Calling devotion from yesterday talked about rest with Jesus a while, that we don't know what lies ahead, but the way we can truly trust Jesus is to enjoy Him moment by moment. Perfect words at a perfect time!

God Bless you all, and THANK, THANK, THANK YOU for all the prayers not only for us, but for all of Colorado... we really need it.

In Jesus' Precious Love,
Kari

P.S. JOKE:
Two guys are talking in a bar. One of them proclaims, "I'm a breast man, myself."
The other replies, "You know, that's awfully sexist!"
The first corrects himself, "You're right. I'm a breast *person*."

- **Written July 4, 2012, 6:42 A.M.**

Happy 4th of July America!

Hoping and praying that you have a blessed day with family and friends.

The Waldo Fires are 75% contained (or higher I missed the news last night), and we had a holy healing rain last night, that hopefully gave the firefighters a reprieve. THANK YOU FATHER GOD! Thank you for your prayers for this fire and for the state of Colorado.

Last weekend we had the opportunity to escape the smoke and the cancer for a few days and head up to the mountains. It was great and what our fam needed before we start this bumpy road. Thank you so much for your prayers, words of encouragement, listening ears, and thank you in advance for all the other ways you will bless our family.

I found a verse the other day in my Jesus Calling, and a friend blessed me with it again last night.

*"**The eternal God is your refuge, and his everlasting arms are under you"** (Deuteronomy 33:27). AMEN!

Surgery still scheduled for Monday the 9th, and chemo to follow 6 weeks or so after.

I don't know what else to say than THANK YOU. You have blessed me and my family so much. Totally overwhelmed by love and prayers and I love how God loves us and uses us to extend His love. Thank you.

Be Blessed and God Bless the U.S.A.

In Jesus' Precious Love,
Kari

- **Written July 9, 2012, 5:23 A.M.: Game Day!**

Thank you, dear family and friends for all your prayers, calls, texts, letters, cards, meals, gifts, love, all of it. Sorry if I missed your call or wasn't able to call you back, please know that you are very much loved and appreciated. God Bless you.

Thank you for your prayers of a good night's rest, I feel rested and energized and excited for this day. In a few hours will be "Game Time," and as my family and I prepare, I want to share with you how God is helping us prepare (thank you to those who have shared with us the following verses and many other treasures from God's word).

1. <u>Full Armor of God</u>— *"Check!"*

"Finally, be strong in the Lord and in his mighty power. Put on the full armor of God, so that you can take your stand against the devil's schemes. For our struggle is not against flesh and blood, but against the rulers, against the authorities, against the powers of this dark world and against the spiritual forces of evil in the heavenly realms. Therefore put on the full armor of God, so that when the day of evil comes, you may be able to stand your ground, and after you have done everything, to stand. Stand firm then, with the belt of truth buckled around your waist, with the breastplate of righteousness in place, and with your feet fitted with the readiness that comes from the gospel of peace. In addition to all this, take up the shield of faith, with which you can extinguish all the flaming arrows of the evil one. Take the helmet of salvation and the sword of the Spirit, which is the word of God. And pray in

the Spirit on all occasions with all kinds of prayers and requests. With this in mind, be alert and always keep on praying for all the Lord's people" (Ephesians 6:10-18 NIV Biblegateway).

2. Prayer, Petition with Thanksgiving—*"Check!"*

"Do not be anxious about anything, but in every situation, by prayer and petition, with thanksgiving, present your requests to God" (Philippians 4:6 NIV Biblegateway)

3. Afraid but Trusting God—*"Check!"*

"When I am afraid, I put my trust in you" (Psalm 56:3 NIV Biblegateway)

4. Peace That Transcends All Understanding—*"Check!"*

"And the peace of God, which transcends all understanding, will guard your hearts and your minds in Christ Jesus" (Philippians 4:7 NLT Biblegateway)

5. Joyful, Praying Continuously, Thankful In All Circumstances—*"Check!"*

"Rejoice always, pray continually, give thanks in all circumstances; for this is God's will for you in Christ Jesus" (1 Thessalonians 5:16-18 NIV Biblegateway).

We totally feel God's love, peace, strength, and comfort surrounding us and He is using you to extend His love to us. Thank you. Our prayer is that as you are praying on our behalf, that the peace of God comes over you. That as you seek Him to intercede for us, you will seek Him with all your heart, and you will find Him—**"You will seek me and find me when you seek me with all your heart"** (Jeremiah 29:13 NIV)—and that you will know His unconditional love, His peace, His strength.

One of my friends made a "super hero" cape for me. She has reminded me that we can all be "super-natural" heroes with God's perfect power.

"But he said to me, 'My grace is sufficient for you, for my power is made perfect in weakness. Therefore I will boast all the more gladly about my weaknesses, so that Christ's power may rest on me.'" (2 Corinthians 12:9 NIV Biblegateway).

Dear Heavenly Father, THANK YOU! I have no words for the peace, strength, and love that I feel and know, except Thank you. I want to Thank You for this day, a day that You made, let us all rejoice and be glad in it. I want to thank You for all the people who are lifting us up in prayer, I pray Father God that You give them a real experience with You today that will bless them. I pray for Dr. L, Dr. G, Nurse R and all the others that will be in the surgery today. May Your love and power be totally represented and extended to those we will meet today. Please be with my family and friends, and give them super-natural strength, peace, love and patience as this day will be long for them. I love You Dear Father and I am so excited to fall into Your arms of comfort and love during this whole experience, thank You that Your everlasting arms are always under me. I praise You Dear Father and give You all the Glory, for this strength is not my own, but it is Yours. I Love You. In Your Precious and Holy Name, Amen.

- **Written July 9, 2012, 11:09 P.M.: Surgery**

   Hello Everyone. Joe here, writing for Kari again...

   As part of Generation X, I'm supposed to feel neither highs nor lows. However, as I write this at the end of a very emotional day, I'm feeling an exuberant joy that only God himself can provide. To sum up three hours of surgery...Kari rocked it. The surgeons removed both breasts and began her reconstruction. But the best news: her lymph nodes were totally clear. (To all ya'll who work in the medical career field...thank you for what you do... truly amazing!) I'm extremely proud of Kari for facing today with boldness and courage. She's in a lot of pain, but has managed to keep her spirits up...and her humor. (When I was relaying to her how many people were praying over her, her reply was "I know...it feels like they're all standing on my chest!") Feistiness is good. Thank you all for supporting us through this ordeal. Today was an important first step and, thank God, everything went pretty well.

- **Written July 11, 2012, 11:20 P.M.**

   Hello all, THANK YOU so much for all your prayers, words of encouragement, calls, texts, everything. I am sorry I have not be able to get to all the calls, texts, e-mails and fb posts, but please know that we appreciate all the love you are pouring out on to us.

Well I have to say my husband is amazing. He truly is. I don't know where I would be without him. Joe gave you an update of the surgery, and how things came out, but I also must add that he rocked it, too. I can't imagine how it felt to be him, and have to wait through the surgery (I am not a patient person). I also can't imagine how hard it is for him to balance being there for his wife, his kids and calling everyone in our family (he is one of 9, + my mom and my 2 bros). Anyway, I've been getting all these accolades and I just wanted to say that Joe has been amazing and really a rock for me. The rock, after Jesus, of course. And when I think about where this strong, courageous man gets all his strength and peace, I know that it is because he leans on Jesus, his Rock of faith. It is hard for anything to steal Joe's joy and he is always displaying that example for me.

Yesterday was a good day, I felt strong, and really confident that I was going to be recovered in a few days.

Today, the "Big-Ole-Mack-Truck" Hit me! I think the OR meds wore off; I was so constipated (sorry, TMI) despite my pro-activeness about making sure this didn't happen; I accidentally erased our whole answering machine (I'm a sap for hanging on to sentimental messages); and I felt like I couldn't do anything and was getting in everyone's way, so I felt helpless. I am a sucky patient. My amazing family that they are just loved me through it all, they even washed my hair, gave me a pedi and hung out with me and took a walk with me. Joe made an amazing home made fresh meal tonight *just because* he thought I would enjoy it. I love that man!

It is amazing how even when we don't feel like praising Jesus, we need to, and how when we do, our hearts and attitudes start changing.

Dear Jesus, I am sorry for the stinking attitude I had this morning, this afternoon and even this evening. I am sorry for not being able to be content in my circumstance of rest. I am sorry I have taken for granted how hard my family is working to take care of me, and I am sorry for feeling sorry for myself because they have to take care of me. Thank You for always giving me a place to fall, and cry out, and kick and scream, and then showing me Your loving ways. Please help me to be more appreciative and loving toward my AMAZING family tomorrow.

"The Lord God is my Strength, my personal bravery, <u>and</u> my invincible army; He makes my feet like hinds' feet and will make me to walk [not to stand still in terror, but to walk] <u>and</u> make [spiritual] progress upon my high places [of trouble, suffering, or responsibility]!" (Habakkuk 3:19 AMP).

- **Written July 18, 2012, 8:33 A.M.: NEW BOOBS!**

Hello Family and Friends,

THANK YOU, THANK YOU, THANK YOU for the way you are blessing my family and me. We are humbled by God's love working through you. Thank you.

Yesterday, I got the bandages off from surgery and one of the four drains removed. I can't tell you how exciting it was to see the surgeons face as he was admiring his work and the healing that is taking place...PRAISE THE LORD!

Speaking of recovery, it has gone a lot better than expected. My range of motion has been surprising, I'm not overdoing it either. Everything is really slow, but the nurse said yesterday that I was doing well and to keep it up. So another PRAISE THE LORD!

I will most likely start chemo on 14 August. Since it's the first one, they told me to expect to be there 6 hours. After that they said it would probably only be 4-5. The good thing is they will be able to do the Herceptin treatment at the same time as the chemo. So when chemo ends (hopefully around thanksgiving time), I will still go in to get Herceptin for a whole year.

Things are good, God is good, and we feel blessed!

Thank you for everything and we love you and are praying for you and your time with God. May you experience Him like you have never experienced Him before.

If I could ask you to please pray for Joe's cousin Lisa and her husband John. John had a brain tumor in September with a not very hopeful prognosis, but he has been a walking miracle. Truly an inspiration to everyone that meets them. Lisa is an amazing woman who has more faith than anyone I know and her attitude toward life and her devotion to Jesus is awe inspiring. Anyway, John has an MRI on Friday to see how things are going. Please keep them in your prayers.

Also please pray for a USAFA classmate's family of Joe and I. Sean Judge passed away a few days ago from a year long battle with cancer. His wife Carmen and children are honoring him tonight at his memorial service in Dublin, OH. Sean's eyes were able to go to a donor yesterday, which is an amazing miracle. Please keep Carmen and children in your prayers, too.

As my Sis-in-love, Lori, always says, "EVERY Breath is a GIFT"!

In Jesus' Precious Love,
Kari

- **Written Jul 26, 2012, 10:19 A.M.**

Dear Family and Friends,

We have been so blessed by all your prayers, thoughts, ears, help, everything you have done to help us through this time of fighting this breast cancer. Thank you.

Last week, Joe and I attended "chemo" class. And truthfully I walked out of there with the wind taken out of my sails. I felt very discouraged at the daunting path ahead. And as I was talking to God about my feelings (Lamentations 2:19; 3:19-33; 3:55-58), He impressed upon my heart: "do not be overcome, but overcome this with My power through prayer." So I quickly got out my notebook and wrote down every common reaction and side effect to the chemo cocktail I will start receiving in a couple of weeks.

For those of you who have asked how you can help me, **this is it!** Please pray against these reactions and side effects. Please pray for me and my family's spirit to be filled with God's joy, please pray for us to wait for hope. If you are not a praying person, I ask you to consider trying to talk to our Heavenly Father, I cannot tell you how overjoyed He will be to hear from you, even if it is on my behalf, and I pray for all of you to really truly experience God in all of this. One of my favorite verses and a life challenge is this: ***"Be joyful always; pray continually; give thanks in all circumstances, for this is God's will for you in Christ Jesus"*** (1 Thessalonians 5:16-18 NIV).

Specific prayer request for chemo, please help us pray against these common reactions and side effects:

Common Reactions:
- **allergic reactions**—rash, itching, trouble breathing, dizziness, fainting, swelling of lips, throat or tongue.
- **edema or fluid retention**—fluid around heart or accumulation in chest.
- **neuropathy**—nerve cells in the hands and feet that stop working properly.
- **liver damage**
- **Stevens-Johnson syndrome or toxic epidermal necrolysis**—serious skin conditions of swelling around the eyes (rare effect).
- **increase risk of infection and bleeding**
- **kidney damage**
- **damage to ear**—hearing loss, dizziness, and loss of balance. Hearing loss in the high frequency and a decreased ability to hear normal conversations.

- **loss of vision**—especially light and colors (rare effect).
- **infusion reaction**—chills, fever, nausea, vomiting, headache, dizziness, shortness of breath, blood pressure changes, weakness and body pain or swelling. Rare effect—lung problems.
- **heart problems**—irregular heart beat. Rare effect—heart failure.

Other Side Effects:
- **anemia**
- **appetite changes**
- **constipation**
- **diarrhea**
- **fatigue**
- **flu-like symptoms**
- **hair loss**
- **mouth and throat changes**
- **pain**
- **sexual changes**
- **skin and nail changes**
- **urinary, kidney and bladder changes**

And although we have taken measures to prevent this, please pray that I don't get pregnant through all of this.

Joe reminds me of this, one of his favorite verses: ***"Therefore I tell you, whatever you ask for in prayer, believe that you've received it, and it will be yours"*** (Mark 11:24 NIV).

"You can pray for anything, and if you have faith, you will receive it" (Matthew 21:22).

So THANK YOU Dear Family and Friends for being Bold and asking for protection for me from the above common reactions and side effects of the chemo. Thank you for praying for my family and our spirits to continue to be filled with joy of the Lord. Our God is much, much bigger than this and even if I experience everything listed above, it wouldn't make a bit of difference (Daniel 3:18), He still is God and will still receive all the glory and praise.

I am scheduled to start chemo 14 Aug. It will be every 3 weeks for 6 treatments. And Lord willing if I am healthy enough to receive all the treatments as scheduled, I will be done the 27th of November, the Tuesday after Thanksgiving....something to truly be thankful for.

Love you and THANK YOU!

In Jesus' Precious Love,
Kari

- **Written August 7, 2012, 10:03 A.M.: Thankful**

Dear Family and Friends,

THANK YOU for your prayers and continued support. I know I will never be able to adequately express the amount of gratitude that my family and I have for what you have and are doing for us. THANK YOU!

I want to thank the Ward Zoo for totally allowing me to have a "cancer-free" break last week in Glenwood Springs.

Thank you for your love, laughter, prayers, tears, and unyielding support. What an amazing experience.

Yesterday I had the opportunity to go to a "Look Good Feel Good" class sponsored by the American Cancer Society. It was enlightening, and I learned a lot, considering I don't usually put on makeup. I met two BEAUTIFUL ladies yesterday that are in their own battles with cancer, and I want to ask you to pray for them. The younger one is very strong and has a great support system. She is engaged, and her whole family shaved their heads in support of her. (Don't worry I won't ask you to do that if I lose my hair:). The older lady, as strong and as beautiful as she is, I felt very sad for her. She has hardly told anyone about her cancer, she made a remark that "she is her own support system." I couldn't imagine doing this without you all! I couldn't imagine doing this without our Heavenly Father. I don't know what her relationship is with Jesus, and I pray that her source of great strength comes directly from Him. But I would like to pray for complete healing of these two beautiful ladies, in God's perfect timing. Thank you.

Want to share a new Spirit of Strength God gave me this weekend in His Holy Perfect True Word: ***"Be strong and courageous, and do the work. Don't be afraid or discouraged, for the LORD God, my God, is with you. He won't leave you or forsake you"*** (1 Chronicles 28:20 Holman Christian Standard Bible).

Thank You Father God that ***"[Your] grace is sufficient for [me]"*** (2 Corinthians 12:9 NIV).

YAY God!

Thank You Dear Ones. Love you and are praying for your time with Our Heavenly Father to be Blessed, Blessed, Blessed!

In Jesus' Precious Love,
Kari

- **Written August 8, 2012, 2:46 P.M.: Green Light, Go!**

Happy Hump Day everyone! Hope this finds you all well. THANK YOU again for all your prayers!

Met with the surgeon today, and he has given me the "green" light to start chemo. (It has been cute listening to him and the oncologist argue over it:). Anyway, so next Tuesday is definitely the day. I also got approved to be part of a clinical trial too. YAY! The clinical trial is testing an alpha inhibitor and a beta blocker on the effects of Herceptin (one of the chemo drugs I will have to take for a year). Herceptin is very hard on your heart, and the 2 drugs being tested are believed to protect the heart against the harsh effects of the Herceptin. It's a win, win for me. If I happen to get one of the drugs, hopefully it will protect my heart. If I get the placebo, I am no better or worse off than the chemo I was scheduled to have. Praying and THANKING God for protecting my heart regardless.

Thank you all for your patience, I know a lot of you have been asking how you can help. Your prayers are amazing, keep them coming. I know when we know what we need, we will ask. Thank you as you continue to let us figure out what we need. THANK YOU!

Love you and God Bless you,

In Jesus' Precious Love,
Kari

P.S. This is one of my favorite turn-that-frown-around verses: ***"'I will forget my complaint, I will change my expression, and smile'"*** (Job 9:27 NIV).

- **Written August 14, 2012, 12:01 A.M.: GO, FIGHT, WIN!**

"First day of chemo, first day of chemo!"

Next week it will be, "First day of school, first day of school" taken from one of my favorite movies, *Finding Nemo*. Which always reminds me of one of my favorite quotes, "Just keep swimming, just keep swimming, just keep swimming..."[18]

I can truly say that I woke up overjoyed and feeling so strong **in God's PERFECT power,** so I am proud to say I must be really weak (2 Corinthians 12:9).

God gave me a verse yesterday that helped me bring a lot of things together for this day, please allow me to share. ***"Train yourself to be godly"*** (1 Timothy 4:7).

How this spoke to me is that we/I, don't automatically react to adversity with joy, yet we/I am commanded by the will of God to **"be joyful always"** (1 Thessalonians 5:16 NIV). We have to put in the training by spending time with God, reading His Perfect and True Word, the Bible, we have to practice and obey His commands and follow His will, we have to make being godly a habit so that the time between adversity striking and being joyful is minimized. We'll never achieve perfectness in this, but we can get closer to it.

How that verse resonated thru me as I remember two very specific verses God gave me early last week. First, **"Be strong and courageous, and <u>do the work</u>. Don't be afraid or discouraged,** [I wish I would have remembered this a few days this weekend.] **for the LORD God, my God, is with you. He will never fail you or forsake you"** (1 Chronicles 28:20, emphasis added). And the other verse: **"I will forget my complaint, I will change my expression, and <u>smile</u>"** (Job 9:27 NIV, emphasis added).

God gave me these verses <u>days before I needed them,</u> yet in the moment of adversity, I failed to be joyful and heed their instruction and obey God...I need a lot more training. Thank You Father God for Your patience with me as I continue to "train myself to be godly."

I really wasn't trying to make this into a Bible lesson, but completely overjoyed with How God works and WHO HE IS, I can't contain it, and wanted to share this, because even in realizing how I fell so short, it was so encouraging to know and see how God is speaking to me, directly, intimately, and even if I miss it, He still did it and I see it in hindsight and that encourages me to pay more attention. How He truly LOVES US, and He is just wanting to share these intimate moments with us, His Presence truly is Heaven.

So completely blessed by all the prayers and thoughts. One sweet friend Julie shared with me to keep "dancing in the rain" and she did not even know that today I woke up so strong in God's perfect power, dancing thru out the day....and it was a perfect rainy day. I LOVE, LOVE, LOVE how God puts the right thoughts in others minds (YOU) and executes PERFECT timing to encourage me. Thank you dear family and friends. We love you and are praying for you. God Bless you.

- **Written August 14, 2012, 6:39 P.M.: Team Ward Round 1 Chemo Done!**

   "Let all that I am praise the LORD;
   with my whole heart, I will praise his holy name.
   Let all that I am praise the LORD;
   may I never forget the good things he does for me.
   He forgives all my sins
   and heals all my diseases.
   He redeems me from death
   and crowns me with love and tender mercies.
   He fills my life with good things.
   My youth is renewed like the eagle's!" (Psalm 103:1-5 NLT Biblegateway).

Round 1 of chemo done! Thank you for all your thoughts and prayers, words of encouragement, and good thoughts. Feeling strong in God's perfect power, and so far so good. BLESSED with all your acts of kindness and love. And praying for you and yours. Thank you. Love you and God Bless you.

- **Written August 22, 2012, 7:38 P.M.**

    "I will praise the LORD at all times.
    I will never stop singing his praises.
    Humble people, listen and be happy,
    while I brag about the LORD.
    Praise the LORD with me.
    Let us honor his name" (Psalm 34:1-3 ERV Biblegateway).

    A week +2 days after first chemo and PRAISE THE LORD, things have been so much better than expected. I am so in awe of our God, He has truly been protecting me from all those side effects.

    Thank you family and friends for all your prayers, thoughts, meals, childcare, cards, acts of kindness, everything. You have allowed me to focus on resting in our LORD, and getting better and that has made all the difference. If I can so humbly and boldly ask, please keep the prayers coming. I had a follow up the other day and the nurse practitioner said from here until the next chemo (4 Sept), I should only feel better.... and right now I feel really good. So again, PRAISE THE LORD!

- **Written August 23, 2012, 6:02 P.M.: The Calm Before the Hairy Storm**

Thank you, thank you, thank you, all for your words of encouragement and prayers. As I sit in anticipation of the whole hair loss thing, I have appreciated advice and humor from some of the warriors that have walked before me. It's not that I'm afraid of being bald, and not that I even have great hair anyway, but it definitely is a different feeling now as I am days away from losing locks, then it was a month ago when I was excited about all the cute hats I was going to get to wear.

No fiery scalp at the moment, but as I was plucking grays out of the top of my head this morning, I did notice how they just jumped out into the tweezers without any resistance. Too bad my leg hairs haven't followed suit. Also noticed that my normal shed of hair, has follicles attached to the end of them.

I have much comfort knowing God knows all the hairs on my head and the ones that will soon be on my floor, in my sink, on my pillow case, in my mouth, etc. Thank YOU God that I am a child of Yours thru faith in Jesus Christ (Galatians 3:26) and **"when I am afraid, I will put my trust in you"** (Psalm 56:3).

The nonprofit, charitable organization Good Wishes sent me a scarf for free, someone hand made it for me, and even embroidered Swarovski crystals on it. What a beautiful and generous treat for my nugget...thank you, Good Wishes. If you know anyone who will be losing their hair to cancer, they are entitled to one free scarf, check out the website: www.goodwishesscarves.org.

God Bless you family and friends, may you be BLESSED! May you have such an amazing God experience today, that you will know that it was none other than our Holy Father God who LOVES YOU!

Love you and praying for you.

In Jesus' Precious Love,
Kari

- **Written August 26, 2012, 9:07 A.M.: Hair on the Brain—Sorry For Another Hair Tale**

   "Faith is the confidence that what we hope for will actually happen; it gives us assurance about things we cannot see" (Hebrews 11:1).

   Let me first say, that what you are about to read may cause you to be upset with me, but I just wanted to be completely transparent and real. I never thought I would spend so much time thinking about this, but even in my struggle to keep my "eye's fixed on Jesus", He somehow manages to teach me a lesson in my distraction...thank You, Jesus!

   It's not that I don't have faith that God could let my hair stay—I have FULL confidence in hoping for that, that it will happen—**IF** it's God's Will. No matter what anybody else says will happen.

My dilemma at the moment is not <u>faith</u>, its <u>will</u>. Is it God's will for my hair to stay? (I know…who really cares!) He is the only one who really knows the answer to that. And the more I delight myself in Him, and as He gives me the desires of my heart (Psalm 37:4), I'm not sure if hanging onto my hair is my desire or if it's pure spite to all those who tell me this "will happen." Terrible huh? Dirty, stinky, rotten, sinning me. My attitude needs some readjustment. Please forgive me as I seek to love on those who haven't exactly rejoiced with God protecting me from the side effects of round one Chemo. But let me assure myself that if it is God's will to work against the side effects of losing my hair, He could do it!

Now it's not that I really want to be bald, but as the days get closer to that realization, I can't seem to get hair off the brain. I don't have fantastic hair anyway, so do I really want to hang onto it? I thought I had nice boobs for a 42-year-old with four previously breast-fed kids, and I didn't even want to hang onto those cancer infected things. So if the Lord God, my God, can allow me no remorse in the loss of a "nice rack," then why haven't I thought that He could also allow me to feel no remorse over a head of stringing-fine-wild hair? I don't know? Maybe my rebellion in spite to all the naysayers that I allowed to demoralize me? I guess my lack of faith that my desires would actually conform to His will. Father God I am sorry.

As I write this, my head still feels normal. The only fiery, itchiness I've experienced has been on my face, and my friend Trina who owns Monumental Microderm, showed me some wash, lotion, and moisturizer from the Reprev line that is taking care of that. At the moment, no clumps of hair, just strand by strand as if God is allowing me to "buy some time" with this process - THANK YOU FATHER! A friend reminded me of this: **"Every good and perfect gift is from above, coming down from the Father"** (James 1:17 NIV). *Oh Father God, how YOU completely Bless and Humble me. I am not even worthy of such a gift, but Your tender mercy is allowing this "soft/sensitive/ emotional" Warrior to process the losing of this crown of locks to the crown of compassion and love (thanks Holly). Thank You Father! I LOVE YOU!*

I know the Father will direct my footsteps if/when it's time for this mane to go. At the moment He is giving me a gift—THANK YOU FATHER! Until that time, and even after, I will continue to delight myself in Him, even if I am a dirty, stinky, rotten sinner. And as I delight in Him, my attitude to spite has disappeared—I'm letting go—all the way up to my follicles:).

God Bless you Dear Ones, and know that I am praying for you, and I am so thankful for your prayers and encouragement.

In Jesus' Precious, Forgiving Love,
Kari

- **Written September 3, 2012, 9:10 P.M.: Estes Park Retreat**

Hey Dear Family and Friends,

It's chemo eve, YUCK! But we just came back from a wkd at Estes Park, and Rocky Mountain National Park. We stayed at the YMCA of the Rockies (GREAT deal and at the entrance of the RMNP). Anyway, we all came back refreshed and ready to hit round 2. Our son even said at lunch today: "Mom, this weekend I forgot you had cancer." YAY GOD!!!!! Perfect weekend!

As we were driving back today, the aspens were starting to change, and Joe and I cranked up a David Crowder Band CD, *Great God*, and a song that resonated thru all of our hearts: "Fall on Your Knees."

Anyway, wanted to share it with you all.

Update on my hair....it died! Literally on my head. No itchies, no fiery scalp, but when I touched it, it broke apart and just started sharding off. It was pretty gross. We had the shaving party, I WILL share pics, I'm just not quite ready or BOLD enough to show the world my bald nugget. Although funny, it has already starting growing back, so I am curious if it will fall out, or just continue to grow. Thanks for all your prayers. LOVE YOU and God Bless you.

In Jesus' Precious Love,
Kari

- **Written September 4, 2012, 5:51 P.M.: Round 2 Done**

It's only hair (an easier statement to say when you actually have some)...thanks for all your prayers, thoughts and encouragement. 20 seconds of courage and bravery is beginning to be a great mantra. I Praise God that even though the hair is not as thick and flowing, short and stubbly for me...He knows every one of them on our heads, or in our laundry.

Round 2 chemo is done, a little tired and not feeling as hot, BUT, I Praise our Lord God, that He is control of everything, and He has given me strength and power and loves us all so very much.

Love to you all, thank you for your prayers.

God Bless you.

P.S. all that you are bringing us food, you ROCK! All have been GREAT, and you must think there are 10 of us, because you have set us up with lots of left overs....THANK YOU! I can honestly say we are good in the food department...anyone want to take our copays? Just kidding (kind of). Anyway, thank you, you all truly BLESS us in all the ways you are helping us!

- **Written September 8, 2012, 7:58 A.M.**

Dear Friends and Family,

Thank you for your continued prayers, love and support. I want to ask you all to pray for Joe's cousin John, he has defeated the odds and so continues to inspire me. Last year John was diagnosed with Glioblastoma and he has fought like a true champion and continues to fight with God's full power, proving that God is much bigger than what any Dr. says or diagnosis gives you. His wife Lisa is an amazing testimony of faith in Christ. Please pray for them,

180

John has an MRI this weekend to help with his upcoming attack plan.

God reminded me this morning of HOW MUCH BIGGER GOD is than any of this. He reminded me that HE is the God who sits on the throne and is in control of it all. YAY GOD!

I have to share with you a lesson God gave me in to-day's devotional *Jesus Calling.* Another perfect timing on God. I don't know why I am ever surprised, HIS TIMING IS ALWAYS PERFECT, THANK YOU Father GOD! Anyway, the author talks about accepting EACH day, EXACTLY how it comes. She reminded me that God will give us the strength moment by moment to deal with anything, and our only job is to completely trust Him.[19] This was such a great thing to read after this last round of chemo.

God is good ALL the time, He continues to love us even when we feel unlovable. He continues to protect and provide for us, even when we feel alone. I am praying for you, that as you pray for me and my family, as you con-tinue to lift up prayers to our Great God, that you may experience His goodness, His love, His faithfulness. He is real and LOVES, LOVES, LOVES YOU!

On a funny, cool "only God could do" note, my hair on my head has started to grow back....I think that is so funny, considering all my leg hair fell out and is gone....YAY what a great gift huh, head locks growing back, no leg hair to shave:)? Some tell me that my hair will fall out of my head again, maybe, I'm just enjoying the little things in life and believing that God can give me some cranial hair if He wants regardless of what chemo is supposed to do:). YAY GOD, YOU ROCK!!!!

- **Written September 14, 2012, 7:16 A.M.: Hiding Place**

"Yet I will rejoice in the LORD!
I will be joyful in the God of my salvation!" (Habakkuk 3:18).

Dear Family and Friends,

THIS is a GREAT day to PRAISE the LORD! Everyday is!

I think I can safely say we made it thru Chemo 2. The other day when I was in my "hiding place" with God, I had this realization that I hadn't prayed against all the negative side effects going into chemo 2. I was apologizing to our Heavenly Father that I took my eyes off of Him, and was focusing on what was "supposed to happen during chemo," and as I pulled out my list, I found myself thanking Him and Praising Him for there were only a few of the side effects on that long list that I had actually experienced. PRAISE THE LORD!

I don't know why I forget HOW powerful of weapon prayer is, or how I forget to prayer for EVERYTHING. I don't know why I forget to BELIEVE that our Heavenly Father, the one who is the Creator of all heavens and earth, the one sitting on the throne, couldn't protect me. But He can if it is His will. Thank You Father and Praise Your Holy Name. We are called to pray without ceasing (1

Thessalonians 5:17), and there is nothing too small or too big that we can't pray to our Heavenly Father about.

Thank you for your continued prayers and thank you to all of you who are continuing to pray against all the negative side effects of chemo for me. 2 down, 4 to go. GO FIGHT WIN! Thank you, you prayer warriors.

I am praying for you to have an AMAZING experience with God our Father in your "hiding place" with Him.

I love you and am so grateful for you. You are blessing our family immensely. Thank you.

God Bless you.

In Jesus' Precious Love,
Kari

- **Written September 17, 2012, 5:26 P.M.**

Great week and feeling good, wanted to ask you all to pray for one of Jonah's former baseball coaches and his family. Scott was diagnosed with a neuroendocrine tumor called a Paraganglioma. He had surgery on the 1 Aug and is recovering from that, he is supposed to have MIBG scan, which is scheduled for tomorrow Tuesday, Sept. 18. This could be a 3-day process: injection of the isotope on Day 1, scan 24 hours later on Day 2, and a possible second scan another 24 hours later on Day 3.

Scott and his wife Jami have 3 small boys, please pray for them. Thank you.

Last night, this passage was part of the message at our church service, had to share it:

"So, chosen by God for this new life of love, dress in the wardrobe God picked out for you: compassion, kindness, humility, quiet strength, discipline. Be even-tempered, content with second place, quick to forgive an offense. Forgive as quickly and completely as the Master forgave you. And regardless of what else you put on, wear love. It's your basic, all-purpose garment. Never be without it. Let the peace of Christ keep you in tune with each other, in step with each other. None of this going off and doing your own thing. And cultivate thankfulness. Let the Word of Christ—the Message—have the run of the house. Give it plenty of room in your lives. Instruct and direct one another using good common sense. And sing, sing your hearts out to God! Let every detail in your lives—words, actions, whatever—be done in the name of the Master, Jesus, thanking God the Father every step of the way" (Colossians 3:12-17 The Message Biblegateway).

- **Written September 24, 2012, 1:54 P.M.**

"Having hope will give you courage.
You will be protected and will rest in safety" (Job 11:18).

A cool amazing verse and promise God gave me this weekend, just in time for chemo 3, and no matter what happens as far as side effects, God is God and He is sitting on His throne and He's got us!

Family and Friends, just wanted to say a big THANK YOU for all your prayers, hugs, smiles, love, texts, e-mails, calls, cards, flowers, meals, kid help, walks, talks, a glass of vino, a margarita and/or beers (the oncologist nurse told me it is definitely ok to have a drink or two or three during chemo:). EVERYTHING! Please know if we don't get back to you right away, or answer your texts or e-mails in a timely manner, we are VERY APPRECIATIVE for all of it. THANK YOU and thanks for your patience and understanding.

We love you and we are praying for you and your time with our Heavenly Father. God Bless you!

In Jesus' Precious Love,
Kari for TEAMWARD

- **Written October 4, 2012, 7:52 A.M.**

This passage is from a devotional called *Streams in the Desert* and has been a great comfort to me the last week (emphasis added):

We are crowded from all sides, *but not defeated...* Without a road, but *not without a 'side road' of escape...*pursued, *but not left alone...*overthrown, *but not overcome...*Yet [I will] not die, for 'the life of Jesus' comes to [my] aid, and [I live] through Christ's life until [my] lifework is complete.[20]

This halfway point in chemo has been rough, but not impossible. At least there is a sick sort of comfort in the cyclical process of chemo. The familiarity with the cycle, not the cycle itself, has brought comfort.

Thank you for your calls, e-mails, texts, cards, prayers, thoughts, everything. I'm sorry if I haven't been able to get to the phone or even return a call or e-mail or text, I am really behind on my correspondence, not sure if I'll ever catch up, but please know your efforts toward loving on us is greatly appreciated.

Love you and God Bless you.

In Jesus' Precious Love,
Kari

April 27, 2012 in San Diego:
the day I noticed the dimple on my left breast. I had no idea how my world was about to change. Those are real boobs, and they tried to kill me!

Notes

(ENDNOTES)

Chapter 1 – *Never Will I Leave You*

[1] Taken from *Jesus Calling: A 365 - Day Journaling Devotional* by Sarah Young Copyright © 2008 by Sarah Young. Used by permission of Thomas Nelson. www.thomasnelson.com. All rights reserved.

[2] Taken from *Jesus Calling: A 365 - Day Journaling Devotional* by Sarah Young Copyright © 2008 by Sarah Young. Used by permission of Thomas Nelson. www.thomasnelson.com. All rights reserved.

[3] Tommy Woodward and Eddie James, *God's Chisel by The Skit Guys* (skitguys.com).

Chapter 2 – *Death by IV*

[4] Jack Nicolson, *The Bucket List* (2007).

[5] Suzanne Collins, *Mocking Jay* (New York: Scholastic Inc., 2010), p.349 and p. 363.

[6] THE GREAT DIVORCE by C.S. Lewis © copyright CS Lewis Pte Ltd 1946.

Chapter 5 – *The 4% Club?*
[7] Herceptin pamphlet about side effects and risks.
[8] PHARE study.

Chapter 7 – *A Dark Deep Pit*
[9] Taken from *Prayers & Promises when facing a life-threatening illness* by Ed Dobson Copyright © 2007 by Ed Dobson. Used by permission of Zondervan. www.zondervan.com. All Rights Reserved.

Chapter 10 – *While I'm Waiting*
[10] Excerpt from UPSIDE-DOWN PRAYERS FOR PARENTS by Lisa T. Bergen, copyright © 2013 by Lisa Tawn Bergren. Used by permission of WaterBrook Press, an imprint of the Crown Publishing Group, a division of Random House LLC. All rights reserved.
[11] Taken from *Jesus Calling: A 365 - Day Journaling Devotional* by Sarah Young Copyright © 2008 by Sarah Young. Used by permission of Thomas Nelson. www.thomasnelson.com. All rights reserved.

Chapter 11 – *Check Engine Light: Service Soon*
[12] Taken from *Jesus Calling: A 365 - Day Journaling Devotional* by Sarah Young Copyright © 2008 by Sarah Young. Used by permission of Thomas Nelson. www.thomasnelson.com. All rights reserved.
[13] Ann Voskamp, *One Thousand Gifts: A Dare to Live Fully Right Where You Are* (Grand Rapids, Michigan: Zondervan, 2010), pp 223-224.

Chapter 13 – *…And Again! Surgery Debacle*
[14] Kirk Cameron, *Unstoppable* (Liberty University: Kirk Cameron Film, 2013).

Chapter 14 – *Be Still, Be Patient, and Wait on the LORD*
[15] Taken from *Encouragement Bible: "Still Waiting: Psalm 40"* Devotion by Dave and Jan Dravecky Copyright © 2001 by Dave and Jan Dravecky. Used by permission of www.Endurance.org. All rights reserved.

Appendix 4 – *The "Backstory" CaringBridge Entries*

[16] Taken from *Crazy Love* by Francis Chan Copyright © 2008 by Francis Chan. Used by permission of David C. Cook. www.davidccook. com. All rights reserved.

[17] Taken from *Jesus Calling: A 365 - Day Journaling Devotional* by Sarah Young Copyright © 2008 by Sarah Young. Used by permission of Thomas Nelson. www.thomasnelson.com. All rights reserved.

[18] Ellen DeGeneres, *Finding Nemo* (2003).

[19] Taken from *Jesus Calling: A 365 - Day Journaling Devotional* by Sarah Young Copyright © 2008 by Sarah Young. Used by permission of Thomas Nelson. www.thomasnelson.com. All rights reserved.

[20] Taken from *Streams in the Desert* by B. Cowman, updated by Jim Reimann Copyright © 1997 by Jim Reimann. Used by permission of Zondervan. www.zondervan.com. All Rights Reserved.

About the Author

Kari L. Ward graduated from the US Air Force Academy with a BS in biology in 1993. She served for twenty years in the US Air Force, with over eight of those years in active duty as a navigator on the KC-135 and the remaining time as an admissions liaison officer for the Air Force Reserves.

Ward married the love of her life, Joe. Together they have four wonderful children. God uses Ward's family to teach her lessons about himself on a daily basis.

Based in the Colorado Springs, Colorado, area, Ward loves God's splendor displayed in the great outdoors. In her spare time, she enjoys camping, hiking, running, swimming, skiing, snowshoeing, biking, cooking, playing guitar, and singing. Ward is also passionate about practicing her Japanese language skills, which she picked up while her family was stationed in Japan.

Made in the USA
Las Vegas, NV
29 January 2022

42586596R00125